Coping with Behavioral Addictions

The Risky Behavior Addiction Workbook

Information, Assessments, and Tools for Managing Life with a Behavioral Addiction

Ester R.A. Leutenberg and John J. Liptak, EdD

Whole Person Associates
Mental Health & Wellness Publishers
Duluth, Minnesota

Whole Person Associates

101 West 2nd Street, Suite 203
Duluth, MN 55802-5004

800-247-6789

Books@WholePerson.com
WholePerson.com

The Risky Behavior Addiction Workbook

Editorial Director: Jack Kosmach
Art Director: Mathew Pawlak
Cover Design: Adam Sippola
Editors: Peg Johnson and Adam Sippola

Library of Congress Control Number: 2022951422
ISBN:978-1-57025-367-6

From the co-authors, Ester and John,
Our gratitude, thanks, and appreciation
to the following professionals:

❧ ○ ❧

Editorial Directors – Jack Kosmach and Peg Johnson

Editor and Lifelong Teacher – Eileen Regen, MEd, CIE

Reviewers – Niki Tilicki, MA Ed and Eileen Jonatis, MA Ed

Proof-Reader –Jay Leutenberg, CASA

Art Director – Mathew Pawlak

❧ ○ ❧

A Special Thank You
to
Whole Person Associates

for their interest in mental health issues.

Free PDF Download Available
To access your free PDF download of the assessment tools
and all of the reproducible activities in this workbook, go to:
https://WholePerson.com/store/TheRiskyBehaviorAddictionWorkbook1422.html

Understanding Behavioral Addictions

There are many types of addictions. The behavioral addictions that are heard about most are substance abuse addictions. However, a behavioral addiction can be the same as a physical dependence on a substance.

> ...it is the compulsive nature of the behavior that is often indicative of a behavioral addiction, or process addiction, in an individual. The compulsion to continually engage in an activity or behavior despite the negative impact on the person's ability to remain mentally and physically healthy and functional in the home and community defines behavioral addiction. The person may find the behavior rewarding psychologically or get a "high" while engaged in the activity but may later feel guilt, remorse, or even be overwhelmed by the consequences of that continued choice. Unfortunately, as is common for all who struggle with addiction, people living with behavioral addiction cannot to stop engaging in the behavior for any length of time without treatment and intervention.

> **~ American Addiction Centers (2019)**

People are increasingly experiencing non-substance behavioral addictions and diminished control over the behavior. Behavioral addictions are no longer categorized as impulse disorders. Behavioral addictions are now viewed as true addictions, much like substance abuse.

The National Institute of Health (2010) states:

> Growing evidence suggests that behavioral addictions resemble substance addictions in many domains, including natural history, phenomenology, tolerance, comorbidity, overlapping genetic contribution, neurobiological mechanisms, and response to treatment.

> ~ Grant et al. 2010

The concept of addiction, for years adopted solely to indicate the use of psychotropic substances, is now being applied to describe a heterogeneous group of syndromes known as 'behavioral addictions,' 'no-drug addictions,' or 'new addictions.' Prevalence rates for such conditions, taken as a whole, are amongst the highest registered for mental disorders with social, cultural, and economic implications. Individual forms of behavioral addictions are linked by a series of psychopathological features that include repetitive, persistent, and dysfunctional behaviors, loss of control over behavior despite the negative repercussions of the latter, compulsion to satisfy the need to implement the behavior, initial well-being produced by the behavior, craving, onset of tolerance, abstinence and, ultimately, a progressive, significant impairment of overall individual functioning.

Why Are They Called Behavioral Addictions?

Behavioral addictions constitute any maladaptive pattern of excessive behavior that manifests in physiological, psychological, and cognitive symptoms such as the following:

- **Continuance:** continuing the behavior despite knowing that this activity is creating or exacerbating physical, psychological, or interpersonal problems.

- **Intention effects:** inability to stick to one's routine, as evidenced by exceeding the amount of time devoted to the behavior or consistently going beyond the intended amount.

- **Lack of control:** unsuccessful attempts to reduce the level of the behavior or cease it for a certain period of time.

- **Reduction in activities:** as a direct result of the behavior, social, familial, occupational, or recreational activities occur less often or are stopped.

- **Time:** a great deal of time is spent preparing for, engaging in, and recovering from the behavior.

- **Tolerance:** increasing the amount of the behavior to feel the desired effect, be it a "buzz" or a sense of accomplishment.

- **Withdrawal:** in the absence of the behavior, the person experiences adverse effects such as anxiety, irritability, restlessness, and sleep problems.

Addiction to Risky Behavior

At some point, all people engage in risky or unwise behaviors. Risky behavior can be defined as any behavior that increases the chance of danger, harm, or unwanted outcomes in the near or distant future (2022 GoodRx Health). People addicted to risky behaviors engage in them because they are exciting, temporarily rewarding, and provide an adrenaline rush (the sudden release of adrenaline). People seek adrenaline rushes that allow them to forget about their problems in life—for a short time. People addicted to risky behavior are often referred to as adrenaline junkies, sensation-seekers, and thrill-seekers. They enjoy intense and thrilling activities that generate an adrenaline rush. These activities could include stealing, fighting, drunk driving, using weapons, risky sex, or more socially acceptable activities like skydiving, bungee jumping, or extreme sports.

It is increasingly recognized that risking or thrilling behaviors have the potential to become addictive. Just as substances such as alcohol and narcotics are habit-forming and addictive, so are risky behaviors. People with an addiction to risky behavior and adrenaline find that their actions can escalate and lead them to spend inordinate amounts of time and money preparing for or engaging in the behavior while neglecting other areas of life.

The problem is that these repetitive, adrenaline-based habits persist even though the person may experience negative consequences. Often, adrenaline addicts think they can control their behavior by allowing themselves an occasional indulgence. However, while these risky behaviors present a temporary buzz, research suggests that people who stop risky behaviors will experience withdrawal symptoms like a person addicted to substances. Eventually, addicted people find they no longer have conscious control over their behavior.

The reason for this withdrawal problem is that people are excited, afraid, or emotionally charged during risky behavior, and their bodies produce adrenaline. When released into the blood, this hormone increases heart rate, blood pressure, and breathing rate, which can sharpen senses and boost energy. People addicted to risky behavior seek this sensation in the same way that substance abusers seek a high from a specific substance

---

RISKY BEHAVIOR ADDICTION IN THE DSM-5

Although absent from the present diagnostic guidelines, such as the World Health Organization (2018) International Classification of Diseases (ICD) and the American Psychiatric Association's (2018) Diagnostic and Statistical Manual of Mental Disorders (DSM-5), experts have recognized that the adrenaline rush associated with risky behavior can quickly and easily become an addiction and lead to physical, occupational, social, and psychological problems.

The way clinicians talk about thrill-seeking includes language that is usually reserved for talking about addiction. But risky and thrill-seeking behavior is not currently classified as an addiction in the Diagnostic and Statistical Manual of Mental Disorders (DSM-5). According to the DSM-5, peer-reviewed research supporting behavioral addictions is still lacking. Some experts have researched the topic of adrenaline rush addiction, and it is set to be included in the next edition of the DSM.

For example, a 2016 study by Heirene, Shearer, Roderique-Davies, and Mellalieu looked at withdrawal symptoms in eight rock climbers. After going through a period of not climbing, participants experienced withdrawal symptoms similar to those experienced by people with addictions to substances.

The overuse and over-indulgence in thrill-seeking and risk-taking behavior can be a behavioral addiction that can be effectively treated using a range of cognitive and behavioral therapies.

Potential Signs of Risky Behavior Addiction

Thrill-seekers and risk-takers share many of the same symptoms as people addicted to substances. They get a rush from thrills and risk-taking behavior, but after a while, they seek out even more dangerous risks to feel that same level of excitement and buzz. Studies indicate that these thrills and risks flood the brain with the same chemicals released by addictive drugs.

People with a risky behavior addiction may experience ...

- A desire for complexity.
- Sensation-seeking thrills.
- Risk-taking that relieves stress.
- Starting arguments for the fun of it.
- Taking a risk after significant problems.
- Engaging in dangerous and unhealthy activities.
- Never saying no to projects, activities, or social events.
- A need to take risks, especially those that seem exciting.
- A dependence on the adrenaline rush received from taking risks.
- Jeopardizing relationships, jobs, or education for the sake of thrills.
- Procrastination on projects to be able to finish them under pressure.
- Taking on more responsibilities and projects when things start to slow down.
- Repeated unsuccessful attempts to control, stop, or reduce risk-taking behaviors.
- The need to lie to conceal risk-taking activity, involvement, or adrenaline rushes.
- Restlessness or irritability when trying to restrict or cut back on risk-taking behaviors.
- A mental preoccupation with risk-taking, such as thinking of ways to increase involvement with the risk.

A Risk-Taking Personality

Thrill-seekers and risk-takers typically have specific personality traits that spark the desire to experience certain sensations and excitement. People drawn and addicted to activities that initiate thrilling sensations and an adrenaline rush have thrill-based personality traits. People differ considerably in their willingness to take risks, and each individual's tendency to take risks will vary.

These traits often include the ...

- Desire for complexity.
- Willingness to take risks.
- Drive to pursue challenges.
- Curiosity about what is next.
- Need for constant excitement.
- Hatred or fear of being predictable.
- Flexibility and openness to change.
- Spontaneity and impulsivity of life.
- Tendency to be outgoing and social.
- Creativity in finding something risky and exciting.
- Pursuit of novel, intense, and complex sensations and experiences.

Thrill-seeking that is mild in nature (like riding a roller coaster) can be fun and not cause problems. However, for people regularly putting their safety and the safety of others in jeopardy, thrill-seeking can cause problems and might mean that they have an addiction to risky behavior.

Risky Behaviors

Risky and thrill-seeking behaviors take many different forms. Blais and Weber (2006) developed the model of domain-specific risk propensity, suggesting that people have varying risk propensity in five categories: financial, recreational, health/safety, ethical, and social. They suggest that people have innate risk thresholds in each area partially depending on the individual's values. When people believe they will benefit from a thrill or risky behavior, they are likely to engage in it. When people do not value the adrenaline rush that follows skydiving, they will be less likely to chase this thrilling or risky behavior.

Following are some risk-taking and thrill-seeking behaviors that fall into each of the above categories:

Financial
- Putting way too much money on a credit card.
- Betting a day's income at a high-stakes poker game.
- Investing more than you can afford in a very speculative stock.
- Putting all of one's money into a risky business venture.
- Gambling.

Recreational
- Skiing down a run that is beyond one's ability.
- Whitewater rafting at high water in the spring.
- Bungee jumping off a tall bridge.
- Skydiving.
- Drag racing.

Health/Safety
- Drinking heavily at a social function.
- Having unprotected sex with strangers.
- Driving a car without wearing a seat belt.
- Riding a motorcycle without a helmet.
- Walking alone at night in an unsafe area of town.
- Mixing multiple drugs or drugs and alcohol for increased effect.

Ethical
- Engaging in aberrant behavior.
- Driving at dangerous speeds.
- Intentionally picking fights with people.
- Engaging in illegal activity, such as stealing or damaging property.
- Lying to or manipulating others for the adrenaline rush or to cover up dangerous behaviors.

Social
- Expressing an unpopular opinion in a work meeting to antagonize your bosses.
- Having sex in public, knowing you might get caught.
- Doing dangerous stunts with friends to try to one-up each other.
- Intentionally starting an argument at a family dinner.

Using This Workbook

The *Risky Behavior Addiction Workbook* provides helping professionals with cognitive and behavioral assessments, tools, and exercises that can be utilized to treat the root psychological causes of an addiction to risky behavior. It helps people identify and change negative, unhealthy thoughts and behaviors that may have led to an addiction to thrill-seeking and sensation-seeking. The activities in this workbook can help participants identify the triggers that can lead to an over-engagement in risky or thrilling behavior and help them discover ways to overcome and manage those triggers.

The *Risky Behavior Addiction Workbook* will help participants to achieve the following:

- Reflect upon the behaviors that were part of the addiction.
- Recognize that they are experiencing an addiction problem.
- Understand the triggers for preoccupation with various aspects of risk.
- Understand recurring patterns that indicate an addiction to risky behavior.
- Learn ways to live a new life without the need to obsess over taking risks.
- Develop greater self-acceptance and the ability to change ineffective behaviors.
- Build self-esteem in positive capabilities outside of risk-taking and sensation-seeking.

The *Risky Behavior Addiction Workbook* is a practical tool for teachers, counselors, and helping professionals in their work with people suffering from risky behavior addiction. Depending on the role of the person using this workbook and the specific group's or individual's needs, the modules can be used individually or as part of an integrated curriculum. The facilitator can administer an activity with a group or individual or use multiple assessments in a workshop..

Confidentiality When Completing Activity Handouts

Participants will see the words **NAME CODES** on some of the activities in the modules. Instruct participants that when writing or speaking about anyone, they should use **NAME CODES** for people to preserve privacy and anonymity. This will allow participants to explore their feelings without hurting anyone's feelings or fearing gossip, harm, or retribution. For example, a friend named **J**ason who **P**lays **V**olleyball **W**ell might be assigned a name code of **PVW** for a particular exercise. To protect others' identities, they will not use people's actual names or initials, only **NAME CODES.**

The Five Modules

This workbook contains five modules of activity-based handouts that will help participants learn more about themselves and their addiction to risk-taking and thrill-seeking. These modules serve as avenues for self-reflection and group experiences revolving around topics of importance in the participants' lives.

The activities in this workbook are user-friendly and varied to provide a comprehensive way of analyzing, strengthening, and developing characteristics, skills, and attitudes for overcoming an addiction to risky behavior.

The activities and handouts in this workbook are reproducible. Minor revisions to suit client or group needs are permitted, but the copyright statement must be retained.

Module 1: Risky Behavior Addiction

> This module helps participants become aware of and explore feelings of being under-stimulated, leading them to compulsive thrill-seeking behavior. They are sensation-seekers or adrenaline junkies who pursue novel and intense experiences without regard for physical, social, lifestyle, or financial risk.

Module 2: Mindfulness of Risky Behavior

> This module helps participants explore mindfulness related to their risky behaviors and adrenaline rush urges. They will learn mindfulness techniques and examine why they live externally, waiting for adrenaline rushes.

Module 3: Adrenaline Need

> This module helps participants examine their need for the adrenaline rush they receive from risk-taking. Adrenaline is produced by any behavior that creates fear or stress. When it becomes an addiction, it can have serious consequences. They will explore why adrenaline is a powerful hormone that propels them into action (fight or flight) when danger is sensed or when preparing for a risky or challenging experience.

Module 4: Risk-Taking Personality

> This module helps participants realize that people addicted to risky behavior often display a personality that will do anything to avoid boredom and experience an adrenaline rush. They learn why this can lead to an addiction. Awareness of these traits can be the starting point of recovery from an addiction to risky behavior.

Module 5: Risk Prevention

> This module helps participants discover the correlation between adrenaline and risk. They will learn that the best way to overcome their addiction to risky behavior is through prevention. They will learn tools and techniques for feeling calm. They are encouraged to reflect upon their lives and actions to discover the source of their addiction to risky behavior and adrenaline.

Different Types of Activity Handouts Included in This Workbook

A variety of materials are included in this reproducible workbook:

- **Action Plans** that assist participants in meeting the goals and objectives of treatment.

- **Assessments** that allow participants to explore their behavior. They can be used again to allow participants to track their progress.

- **Drawing and Doodling** allow participants to unleash the power of the right side of the brain.

- **Educational Pages** that provide insights and tips related to the topic.

- **Group Activities** to encourage collaboration among participants.

- **Journaling Activities** can help participants clarify their thoughts and feelings, thus gaining helpful self-knowledge.

- **Quotation Pages** allow participants to reflect on many powerful quotes and determine how they apply to their lives.

- **Tables** that require participants to reflect on their lives in the past, understand themselves in the present, and react more effectively in the future.

References

American Addiction Centers (2019). Behavioral Addictions. https://americanaddictioncenters.org/behavioral-addictions

American Addiction Centers (2019). Project Know.com https://www.projectknow.com/behavioral-addictions/

American Psychiatric Association (2018). Diagnostic and Statistical Manual of Mental Disorders (DSM–5), https://www.psychiatry.org/psychiatrists/practice/dsm

Association For Consumer Research. https://www.acrwebsite.org/volumes/eacr/vol8/eacr_vol8_71.pdf

Blais, A.R., & Weber, E.U. (2006). A Domain-Specific Risk-Taking (DOSPERT) scale for adult populations. Judgment and Decision Making, vol. 1, no. 1, pp. 33-47. http://journal.sjdm.org/06005/jdm06005.htm

GoodRx Health (2022). https://www.goodrx.com/well-being/addiction/risky-behavior

Grant, J. E., Potenza, M. N., Weinstein, A. & Gorelick, D. A. (2010). Introduction to Behavioral Addictions. *American Journal of Drug and Alcohol Abuse, 36(5), 233–241.*

Heirene, R.M., Mellalieu, S.D., Roderique-Davies, G., and Shearer, D. (2016). Addiction in Extreme Sports: An Exploration of Withdrawal States in Rock Climbers. Journal of Behavioral Addictions Vol. 5, no. 2.

National Institute of Health (2010). Introduction to Behavioral Addictions. https://www.ncbi.nlm.nih.gov/pmc/articles/PMC3164585

World Health Organization (2018). International Classification of Diseases (ICD) Information Sheet. https://www.who.int/classifications/icd/factsheet/en/

Table of Contents

(Continued on page xiii)

Table of Contents

(Continued on page xiv)

Table of Contents

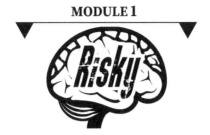

Risky Behavior Addiction

Name _____

Date _____

Risky Behavior Addiction Assessment
Introduction and Directions

Adrenaline is a naturally produced hormone that the body releases when experiencing an intense emotion, or when a "fight or flight" response is triggered. This can result in a rush (or high) which can become addictive for some people.

A person who feels under-stimulated and compulsively engages in thrill-seeking, always looking for novel experiences, may have an addiction to risky behavior. People who compulsively pursue an adrenaline rush are known as sensation-seekers or adrenaline junkies. Sensation-seeking behavior is the pursuit of novel and intense experiences without regard for physical, social, lifestyle, or financial risk.

The *Risky Behavior Addiction Assessment* contains 32 statements that will help you to explore the types of sensations you seek the most.

Read each statement and decide whether or not the statement describes you. If the statement describes you, place a checkmark in the box in front of the statement. If the statement does not describe you, leave the box in front of the statement empty.

In the following example, the first statement is descriptive of the person completing the assessment, but the second is not:

How many of these would you like to do?
- ☑ Betting way too much.
- ☐ Risking a day's income at a high-stakes poker game.

This is not a test. Since there are no right or wrong answers, do not spend too much time thinking about them. **BE HONEST!**

If you choose, no one else needs to see the results.

(Turn to the next page and begin.)

Risky Behavior Addiction Assessment

Name _____ Date _____

This will only be accurate if you respond honestly. No one else needs to see this if you choose.

How many of these would you like to do?

☐ Betting way too much.
☐ Risking a day's income at a high-stakes poker game.
☐ Investing in a speculative stock.
☐ Jumping into a new business venture without checking it out.
☐ Going on a shopping spree.
☐ Making a purchase on a credit card with no money available to pay for it.
☐ Maintaining a high-risk investment in a retirement portfolio.
☐ Taking unpredictable risks in hope of financial rewards.

Financial Risk TOTAL = _____

☐ Engaging in unprotected sex with strangers.
☐ Driving a car without wearing a seat belt.
☐ Riding a motorcycle without a helmet.
☐ Driving a car while drinking an alcoholic beverage.
☐ Going down a ski run that is beyond my ability.
☐ Whitewater rafting at high water in the spring.
☐ Bungee jumping off a tall bridge.
☐ Skydiving.

Physical Risk TOTAL = _____

☐ Engaging in aberrant behavior.
☐ Drinking heavily at a social function.
☐ Hiring a sex worker.
☐ Driving well above the speed limit, with or without other people in the car.
☐ Mixing multiple drugs, or drugs and alcohol, for an increased effect.
☐ Intentionally picking fights with anyone.
☐ Working all the time while neglecting family.
☐ Engaging in illegal activity like stealing or damaging property.

Lifestyle Risk TOTAL = _____

☐ Choosing a career that sounds like fun over a more secure one.
☐ Having an affair with a married person.
☐ Vehemently speaking my mind about an unpopular issue in a meeting at work.
☐ Lying, manipulating, or covering up possible dangerous behaviors just for the adrenaline rush.
☐ Angrily disagreeing with the boss on a significant issue.
☐ Arguing when my tastes are different from those of a friend or acquaintance.
☐ Moving to a country far away from my extended family and from everyone I know.
☐ Changing careers constantly, without funds to support a family.

Social Risk TOTAL = _____

Go to the next page for scoring assessment results, profile interpretation, and individual description.

Risky Behavior Addiction Assessment

Scoring Directions and Profile Interpretation

The assessment you just completed is designed to measure the most prominent risks contributing to your addictive behavior.

Count the number of items you checked in each section of the Risky Behavior Addiction Assessment. Put that total on the line marked TOTAL on the assessment at the end of each section. Then, transfer your totals to the spaces below:

Financial Risk TOTAL   =   _____

Physical Risk TOTAL   =   _____

Lifestyle Risk TOTAL   =   _____

Social Risk TOTAL   =   _____

Assessment Profile Interpretation

By checking even ONE statement, the assessment indicates that you are presently experiencing problems due to an addiction to risky behavior. The more items you checked, the greater your risk of experiencing many problems due to your risky behavior addiction.

On each continuum line, place an X to represent how many items you checked on the assessment.

FINANCIAL RISK (Risk-taking with your money)

0 = Low	4 = Moderate	8 = High

PHYSICAL RISK (Risk-taking with your body)

0 = Low	4 = Moderate	8 = High

LIFESTYLE RISK (Risk-taking with your lifestyle)

0 = Low	4 = Moderate	8 = High

SOCIAL RISK (Risk-taking with your interactions)

0 = Low	4 = Moderate	8 = High

Identify the Symptoms

The body already produces adrenaline, so it may be difficult to recognize the addictive effects. The best way to see if you have a risky behavior addiction may be to stop all activity and see how you feel. If you normally go rock climbing or speed while driving, stop the activity for several days. People addicted to risky behavior usually have adrenaline withdrawal symptoms when unable to engage in their usual stimulating or high-risk activities.

After you have tried to stop, or if you have already tried to stop at some time in the past, respond to the questions below to gauge your withdrawal symptoms.

Risky behavior I will stop: _____

Describe your attempts to stop the behavior. How successful were you?

_____

_____

How did you feel emotionally?

_____

_____

What physical problems did you notice?

_____

_____

How did you experience stress and anxiety?

_____

_____

What conclusions did you come to after identifying the symptoms and responding above?

_____

_____

How I Feel

Adrenaline "junkies" often engage in risky behavior when they feel bored, restless, or under-stimulated. They find themselves bored with what ordinary people would consider intense or stimulating experiences, and they seek higher levels of sensation.

In the spaces that follow, identify the times you sought sensation and took risks.

Times I Engaged In Risk-Taking Behavior	What I Was Feeling	The Outcome Of My Behavior
Example: I went bungee jumping off the tallest bridge in my town.	*I was bored at home and feeling stress about a work project.*	*The thrill of the jump took away my boredom and I forgot about work for a little while.*

Adrenaline has always been my thing.
~ Tom Holland

My Risks

People with an addiction to risky behavior tend to take risks that are often unhealthy in many ways. The risks might be financial, physical, social, or lifestyle.

In the hexagons below, list some of the most prominent risks you take. On the lines next to each, write about why you like to take risks in those areas.

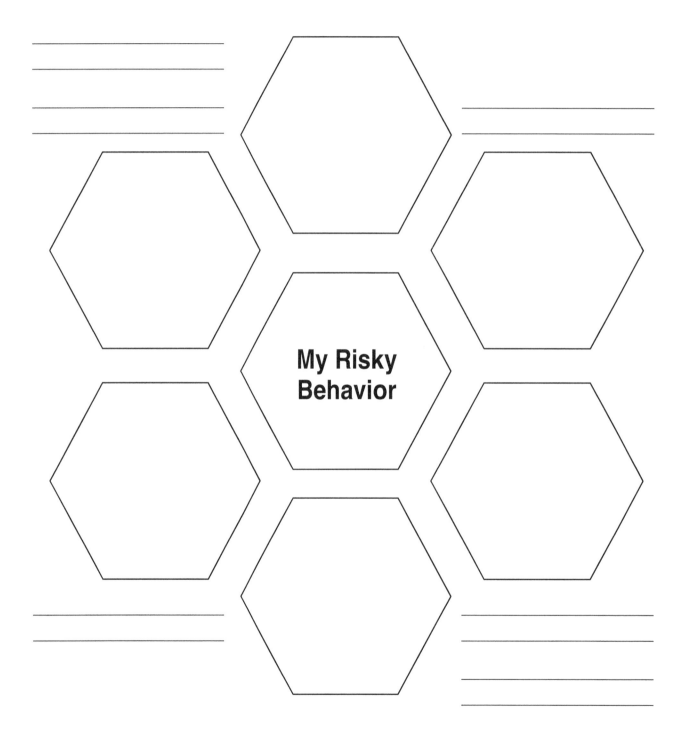

My Risky Behavior

Reduce Sensation-Seeking

When you feel the urge to seek sensations, immediately address the urge.

Here are three ways to do this!

Mindfulness: Stay in the present to temper thoughts of risk-taking. Focus your awareness on the present moment while calmly acknowledging and accepting your feelings, thoughts, and bodily sensations.

Relaxation: Calm yourself by focusing on your breathing, being mindful of your internal senses and surroundings, and visualizing a calm, quiet place. Stay in that place until the adrenaline rush urge diminishes.

Exercise: Rather than giving in to your risky behavior urge, you can go to the gym, walk your pet, practice martial arts, lift weights, jog, etc.

Below, write about how you have used coping mechanisms to battle sensation-seeking urges.

Mindfulness:

Relaxation:

Exercise:

Substitute When Possible

One way to deal with sensation-seeking urges is to substitute a healthy, risk-free activity instead of engaging in risky behavior.

List your sensation-seeking behaviors and identify some healthy substitutes you can use.

Sensation-Seeking Behaviors	My Healthy Substitutes
Example: Openly carrying my gun in public.	*Only using my firearm at the firing range.*

How can you turn one or more of these substitutions into a permanent habit?

_____

_____

_____

_____

My Risks and Consequences

People addicted to the adrenaline rush from thrilling behaviors seek risks to maintain an adrenaline buzz. Think about some of the risks you have experienced and define the consequences.

Write a letter to someone you love, preferably someone still in school, to warn them about the negative consequences of risk-taking.

Dear_____

I want to share some of my experiences with you because I care about you and your future.

_____

_____

_____

_____

_____

_____

_____

_____

_____

_____

_____

_____

_____

_____

Signed, your_____

Sensation-Seeking Behavior

Sensation-Seeking Behavior: the pursuit of novel and intense experiences without regard for physical, social, lifestyle, or financial risk.

If you are addicted to risky behavior, you will feel sensation-seeking urges. What types of things do you feel the urge to do?

In the boxes below, identify the risk-taking behaviors you desire the most. In the space next to each box, list when you get the risk-taking urges most often.

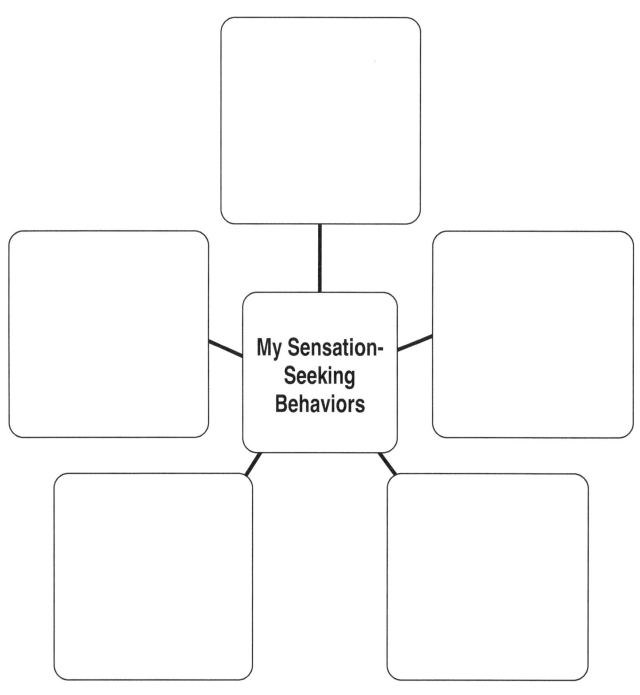

Distract Yourself

People who are addicted to the rush from thrill-seeking may suddenly feel an urge to engage in risky behavior. It is important to learn methods to distract yourself when you become bored or feel an urge.

Below, identify some of the ways you have tried to distract yourself. How can you be more successful?

Ways to Distract Myself	How Successful Were You If You Tried? If You Did Not Try, Why Didn't You?	How I Can Be Even More Successful.
Example: Go for a Walk	*When I begin to feel the urge to gamble, I have tried to take my dog to the park for a walk. It works!*	*Make walking a daily part of my routine. It could be something to look forward to, rather than just a distraction.*
Go for a Walk		
Meditate		
Engage in a Hobby		
Socialize		
Journal		
Exercise		
Breathwork		
Do Yoga		
Other		

All profound distraction opens certain doors. You have to allow yourself to be distracted when you are unable to concentrate.
~ Julio Cortázar

How does the above quote apply to you? _____

_____

_____

My Risk-Taking Journal

Journaling can help you become more mindful of your risk-taking behavior. It will focus your thoughts on the events of the day by recording your risky habits, the time of day when you had urges, and how you felt emotionally during these times.

On the Sensation-Seeking chart below, track your risk-taking habits for a week.

Day of the Week	Time	Risk-Taking Habit	Risk-Taking Emotional Feelings
Example: Monday	*3:00 PM*	*I was at work. I became tired. I snuck away with my co-worker for a little love-making in the janitor's closet.*	*I felt excited and turned on. After, I felt anxious and afraid to go home. My wife called while I was away from my desk and then asked to speak to my co-worker. I think she knows what I did.*
Monday			
Tuesday			
Wednesday			
Thursday			
Friday			
Saturday			
Sunday			

You can reproduce this page and continue to journal in the future!

Thrill-Seeking Triggers

Urges to seek a thrill and take a risk can come on at any time. It is vital for people addicted to the rush of risky behavior to be aware of the time, place, and people involved in their triggers.

Below, write about when you feel triggered to seek thrills and take risks.

My Trigger	When I Was Triggered	Where I Was	What I Did	Outcome
Example: I was bored and felt an urge for excitement.	*Sunday night when everyone was busy.*	*At home.*	*I went bungee jumping. It was exhausting. I didn't get home until after 2 am.*	*I was not productive at work the next morning, and my boss noticed!*

What did you learn?

_____

_____

Things to remember:
- Try to identify where these triggers originated.
- Reframe negative beliefs by beginning with one trigger with the least emotional charge and slowly reprograming it compassionately.
- Act as if the reframing is already working for you, which will help your subconscious mind accept it.

No, No, No, No!

One aspect of risky behavior addiction is that you often have many ways to fulfill sensation-seeking urges. For example, if you get an adrenaline rush from taking financial risks, you might gamble, make aggressive online investments, overspend, etc.

In the four spaces below, write about, draw, or doodle up to four ways you have difficulty saying "NO!" to your urges to engage in risky behavior.

I have a difficult time saying NO to my urges when …	I have a difficult time saying NO to my urges when …
I have a difficult time saying NO to my urges when …	I have a difficult time saying NO to my urges when …

Risk-Taking Reflection

People with an addiction to risky behavior must continuously deal with their urges.

On the line under each statement about risky behavior, place an X on the continuum. On the dotted line below each one, write why you rated yourself that way. **BE HONEST!**

I am obsessed with taking risks.

0 (Not Much)   5 (A Little)   10 (A Great Deal)

I keep taking risks even when I know they are bad for me.

0 (Not Much)   5 (A Little)   10 (A Great Deal)

My risks control my life.

0 (Not Much)   5 (A Little)   10 (A Great Deal)

I cannot fight my risk-taking urges.

0 (Not Much)   5 (A Little)   10 (A Great Deal)

I take risks when a problematic situation happens in my life.

0 (Not Much)   5 (A Little)   10 (A Great Deal)

The HIGHER your score on each of the statements above, the more of a problem you have in that aspect. Areas where you scored low suggest you are not experiencing many signs of addiction in those areas. Remember circling even ONE answer can indicate you might be at risk for experiencing harmful effects on your personal and professional lives.

How much will your life change if you overcome your addiction to risk-taking?

0 (Not Much)   5 (A Little)   10 (A Great Deal)

Do you want to change your current risk-taking habits?

0 (Not Much)   5 (A Little)   10 (A Great Deal)

Work and Play

People addicted to the rush associated with risky behavior are often drawn to incredible work and play activities.

Answer the following questions to see how drawn you are to risky work and play activities.

Are you drawn to extreme sports or activities (rock climbing, bungee jumping, skydiving, riding a motorcycle, racing cars, skateboarding, MMA fighting, traveling to unsafe areas, snowboarding, or anything that could be considered a dangerous or risky activity)? ***List them in the box below and indicate what you like about each of them.***

Are you drawn to particularly dangerous lines of work or a high-stress job, such as a firefighter, police officer, CEO, etc.? ***Write about them in the box below.***

Are you willing to take major risks to your health and safety to experience something new and exciting? ***Write about them in the box below.***

Admit It! You are Addicted

Like any other addiction, real change cannot occur until you admit you have a problem with risky behavior. Not only do you need to acknowledge that you have an issue, but you also need to have a sincere desire to fix the problem.

Complete the sentence starters below and then explain how you will work to overcome your risky behavior activities.

Regarding my risky behavior, I am addicted to _____

I will attempt to overcome this addiction by _____

_____

_____

I have a difficult time controlling my addiction because _____

_____

_____

I will try to overcome this addiction by _____

_____

_____

I wish I could control this urge by _____

_____

_____

I love an adrenaline rush because _____

_____

_____

I will overcome this addiction by _____

_____

_____

Once you have acknowledged your risky behavior problem and decided to overcome it, seek counseling from a mental health professional to help you recover from your addiction.

Limit Thrill-Seeking

Risky behavior addicts may find themselves craving extreme, high-risk, or sensational activities. What sets thrill-seeking people apart from others is that they crave these novel and intense experiences despite the physical or social risks. To beat your addiction, you must limit how often you engage in these thrill-seeking activities.

Explain how you will limit your thrill-seeking behaviors below.

Experience Seeking: You enjoy new, complex, and intense sensations and experiences.

_____

_____

Thrill and Adventure Seeking: You enjoy moderately frightening activities and seek out physical activities that are exciting and risky.

_____

_____

Disinhibition: You like to be spontaneous and search for opportunities to lose your inhibitions (inner mechanisms that forbid or restrict) without consideration of potential consequences.

_____

_____

Boredom: You become bored quickly and cannot tolerate the absence of external stimuli.

_____

_____

Reasons people seek sensations

To get in the flow. Are there other ways you can get in the flow that are not so risky?

_____

_____

To get a buzz. Are there ways you can get a buzz without taking a risk?

_____

_____

Quotes about Sensation-Seeking

Read all three of the quotations below.

#1

The thirst for powerful sensations takes the upper hand both
over fear and over compassion for the grief of others.
~ Anton Chekhov

#2

I'm one of these people that likes an adrenaline rush and new things,
like extreme sports. It makes me feel alive.
~ Gisele Bundchen

#3

Choosing to avoid uncomfortable feelings offers immediate short-term relief,
but avoidance can lead to long-term consequences.

~ Amy Morin

Pick a quote that sounds like you and explain why. #_____

_____

_____

Pick one that inspires you to do better and explain how you will do that. #_____

_____

_____

Pick a quote that taught you something and explain what it taught you. #_____

_____

_____

Write your very own quote regarding sensation-seeking behaviors.

_____

_____

_____

_____

_____

_____

The Risky Behavior Addiction Workbook — **RISKY BEHAVIOR ADDICTION**

38   © 2023 WHOLE PERSON ASSOCIATES, 101 WEST 2ND STREET, SUITE 203, DULUTH MN 55802 • 800-247-6789 • WHOLEPERSON.COM

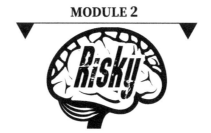

Mindfulness of Risky Behavior

Name _____

Date _____

39

Mindfulness Assessment
Introduction and Directions

Many people with an addiction to risky behavior are not mindful of the moment they are experiencing an adrenaline rush urge, nor do they even realize that they have a problem. They live externally, waiting for the next adrenaline rush. Awareness and mindfulness are often the starting point of recovery.

The *Mindfulness Assessment* contains 15 statements related to your mindfulness. This assessment will help you to gauge your level of mindfulness.

Read each of the statements and decide whether they describe you.
- *If it clearly describes you, circle the number in the VERY column next to that item.*
- *If it describes you a little, circle the number in the SOMEWHAT column next to that item.*
- *If it does not describe you, circle the number under the NOT column next to that item.*

In the following example, the circled number 1 indicates the statement does not describe the person completing the inventory:

Related to my awareness of adrenaline sensations and risk-taking behavior ...

	VERY	SOMEWHAT	NOT
I can stay in the present most of the time	3	2	(1)

This is not a test. Since there are no right or wrong answers, do not spend too much time thinking about them. **BE HONEST!**

If you choose, no one else needs to see the results.

(Turn to the next page and begin.)

Mindfulness Assessment

Name _____ Date _____

This will only be accurate if you respond honestly. No one else needs to see this if you choose.

Related to my awareness of adrenaline sensations and risk-taking behavior ...

	VERY	SOMEWHAT	NOT
I can stay in the present most of the time	3	2	1
I dwell a lot on the past	3	2	1
I always worry about what is going to happen next	3	2	1
I have a problem bringing my thoughts back to the present	3	2	1
I try to be aware of my negative thoughts	3	2	1
I use my senses to bring me back to the present	3	2	1
I am not observant of my surroundings	3	2	1
I can easily remain positive	3	2	1
I create reminders to bring me back to the present	3	2	1
I can focus on only one task at a time	3	2	1
I am unaware of my adrenaline rush urges	3	2	1
I understand my feelings and bodily sensations	3	2	1
I observe my breathing	3	2	1
I pause between thoughts and actions	3	2	1
I maintain awareness at all times	3	2	1

Mindfulness TOTAL = _____

Go to the next page for scoring assessment results, profile interpretation, and individual description.

Mindfulness Assessment

Scoring Directions and Profile Interpretation

The assessment you completed measures how well you stay in the present without dwelling on the past or projecting yourself into the future.

Count the numbers you circled on the Mindfulness Assessment. Put that total on the line marked TOTAL at the end of the section on the assessment. Transfer your total to this space below:

Mindfulness TOTAL = _____

Assessment Profile Interpretation

Place an X on the line to represent your score.

15 = Low	30 = Moderate	45 = High

LOW scores (15 – 25) suggest you are not very mindful.

AVERAGE scores (26 – 36) suggest you are mindful some of the time.

HIGH scores (37 – 45) suggest you are mindful most of the time.

What is your reaction to your score?

_____

_____

Look at the statements again on the assessment. How can you be more mindful?

_____

_____

Reliving Adrenaline Rushes

Many people with an addiction to risky behavior spend a lot of time thinking about the past and reliving old risks, thrills, and adrenaline rushes.

Explore your past risky behaviors and adrenaline rushes. Why do you continue to focus on them, and how can you be more mindful in the present moment?

Past Risky Behaviors And Adrenaline Rushes	Why I Focus on It	How I Can Be More Mindful in the Present
Example: I went skydiving once. It was scary and thrilling all at the same time!	*It gives me something to impress people with, and when I tell the story, I relive it and want to do it again!*	*Notice my desire to impress and instead be with the sensations in my body related to that desire.*

Mindfulness Tip: Whenever you become distracted or notice an urge for an adrenaline rush coming on, focus your attention on your breath, specifically the rise and fall of your chest. When the urge passes, use your breath to anchor your mind and maintain awareness of the present moment.

Anticipating Risky Behavior

Many people addicted to risky behavior spend a lot of time thinking about the future and preparing for their next risky behavior and adrenaline rush. *Example: You might keep thinking about, talking about, and preparing for your next skydiving outing.*

Explore your future risky behavior and adrenaline rushes, why you continue to focus on them, and how you can be more mindful in the present moment.

Past Risky Behavior	The Reasons I Focus on This So Often	How I Can Be More Mindful
Example: I had a one-night stand with my partner's best friend.	*I remember it being so exciting, but I felt guilty and told my partner, who then left me.*	*I need to consider the possible consequences. At the time, I didn't realize I'd feel guilty, or my partner would be hurt and react that way.*

Mindfulness Tip: Try doing a body scan, which involves scanning your body from head to toe to become aware of any discomfort, sensations, or urges. These could be related to anxiety and stress and signal that you will soon get an urge to engage in risky behavior.

Reducing Thrill-Seeking Urges

People addicted to thrill-seeking need the buzz they receive when they give in to their urges. One of the most important aspects of dealing with a risky behavior addiction is to reduce and manage these urges. You may be able to do this by physical exercise, a walk in the park, a jog with a friend, a long shower, deep breathing, reading a book, going to the movies alone, meditating, or talking to a trusted friend or counselor.

What are some of the ways you have unsuccessfully dealt with your urges for thrill-seeking, as well as some of the ways you have successfully dealt with them?

Unsuccessful Ways I Have Dealt with Thrill-Seeking Urges	Successful Ways I Have Dealt with Thrill-Seeking Urges

Avoided Emotions

People addicted to risky behavior are not always mindful of what is occurring in the present moment. When they are not mindful, they are unaware of the variety of emotions they are experiencing. Living for adrenaline rushes can be a severe problem in life if it's to avoid such emotions as guilt, shame, depression, anxiety, frustration, agitation, etc.

Dig deeply. Think about the emotions you avoid. When do you experience these feelings, and how can you be more aware? Use what you learn to complete the table below.

Emotions I Avoid	When I Experience These Feelings	How I Can Be More Aware
Example: Anxiety	*When I try to stop my risky behavior at the request of the supportive people in my life.*	*Get curious about the connection between my anxiety and stopping my risky behavior.*

Mindful Muscle Relaxation
- Focus on your breathing. Slow, even, regular breaths. Breathe in relaxation and breathe out tension. Breathe in relaxation and breathe out tension. Continue to breathe slowly and rhythmically.
- Relax by letting all the tension go in your toes. Feel the muscles going limp, loose, and relaxed. Notice how comfortable the muscles feel now. Now do the same with your feet, ankles, calves, keeping them relaxed. Continue onto your thighs and then buttocks. Work your way up to your stomach, chest, arms, hands, fingers, shoulders, neck, mouth, eyelids, and the top of your head.
- Allow any last bits of tension to drain away. Notice your calm breathing. Enjoy the relaxation for a few moments. When you are ready to return to your usual level of alertness and awareness, slowly begin to re-awaken your body.
- Wiggle your toes and fingers. Swing your arms gently. Shrug your shoulders. Stretch if you like.

Adrenaline Triggers

People addicted to the adrenaline rush their risky behaviors provide can develop an awareness of their triggers.

On the line under each of the ways you might experience triggers, place an X on the continuum indicating how much you relate to each statement. On the dotted line below each one, write why you rated yourself that way. **BE HONEST!**

I feel an increase in my heart rate when I have an urge to take a risk.

0 (Not Much)   5 (A Little)   10 (A Great Deal)

I experience rapid breathing when I have an urge to take a risk.

0 (Not Much)   5 (A Little)   10 (A Great Deal)

I feel my skin sweating when I have an urge to take a risk.

0 (Not Much)   5 (A Little)   10 (A Great Deal)

I begin breathing rapidly when I have an urge to take a risk.

0 (Not Much)   5 (A Little)   10 (A Great Deal)

The HIGHER your score on each of the scales above, the more of a problem you have in the specific aspect measured by the assessment. Areas where you scored low suggest that you are not experiencing many triggers of an adrenaline rush in those areas.

How will your life change if you overcome your addiction to adrenaline?

0 (Not Much)   5 (A Little)   10 (A Great Deal)

Do you want to change your current risk-taking habits?

0 (Not Much)   5 (A Little)   10 (A Great Deal)

Awareness of My Problem

The first and most significant step to overcoming an addiction to risky behavior is to become aware and admit that you have a problem. It takes tremendous strength and courage to own up to this, especially if you are not mindful of how your risk-taking behavior hurts you and your loved ones.

On each of the sentence starters below, explore how you are aware of your addiction to risky behavior and describe how you will be more mindful in the future.

I am aware I have a problem because _____

_____

I will be more mindful of it by_____

_____

I am aware I have a problem because _____

_____

I will be more mindful of it by_____

_____

I am aware I have a problem because _____

_____

I will be more mindful of it by_____

_____

I am aware I have a problem because _____

_____

I will be more mindful of it by_____

_____

I Take Risks When ...

It is essential to be mindful of the times that you take unhealthy risks! What prompts your behavior? Are you stressed? Do you want to forget something negative that has happened? Do you miss someone? Are you bored? Are the urges at particular times of the day or night? Certain days of the week? When are you stressed?

Below, explore the destructive habitual patterns of your risky behaviors.

Awareness of My Risk-Taking Urges	My Behaviors	How I Can Change the Pattern
Example: Time of Day	*I cannot sleep, so I search for porn at 2 am.*	*I will stop looking at porn at late hours and will develop better sleep habits.*
Time of Day		
Where I Am		
What I Am Doing		
Day of the Week		
Who I Am With		
What I Am Stressed About		
What Is Occurring in Life		
What I Am Thinking About		
Other		

Mindfulness means being awake. It means knowing what you are doing.
~ Jon Kabat-Zinn

My Adrenaline Rush

One of the most critical aspects of overcoming an addiction to risky behavior and adrenaline is to identify your adrenaline rushes and take them out of your subconscious into your daily awareness.

Complete the following sentence starters to explore further and become more mindful of who and what triggers your adrenaline rushes and your need to engage in risky behavior.

I get an adrenaline rush when I _____

_____

_____

_____

I get an adrenaline rush when I am_____

_____

_____

_____

I get an adrenaline rush when I am with _____

_____

_____

_____

I get an adrenaline rush when I think about _____

_____

_____

_____

I get an adrenaline rush when I engage in recreational activities such as _____

_____

_____

_____

I get an adrenaline rush when I am feeling_____

_____

_____

_____

Emotions, Thoughts, and Actions

Being more aware of the interaction of your emotions, thoughts, and actions is crucial. All three are intricately linked.

Identify the cause and effect of the link between your emotions, thoughts, and actions.

Emotion I Have Experienced	Thoughts That Followed the Emotion	Actions That Followed the Emotion and Thoughts
Example: I get mad when my partner talks about saving money for retirement.	I think my partner is criticizing me and how I deal with money.	I go online to change my retirement investments so they are riskier than before.

Mindfulness Tip: One way to be more mindful is to stop the negative thoughts that run through your head. Reframing these thoughts or putting a positive spin on them can help you accept and change them more easily. It is essential to be aware of and acknowledge your negative thinking and then reframe your thoughts so you can stay detached and not allow negative thoughts to affect you adversely.

Think Like a Detective

People who have an addiction to risky behavior are often unaware of the unrealistic thoughts that pass through their heads. These thoughts can be related to sensation-seeking. *(For example: let's have a thrill tonight!)* Or they can be related to a problem in your life. *(You will never be promoted to manager, so you may as well...)* Both of these types of thoughts will prompt you to seek risks and thrills.

An example:

- *Unrealistic thought: If I play just one more round on this video game, I'll set a new record.*
- *Feelings that follow: I feel excited and determined to keep playing until I set a record.*
- *Where is the evidence that this is true? Actually, I've been thinking it for an hour. It hasn't happened.*
- *More realistic thinking: I've already been playing for 3 hours. I can play again another day. A break would be wise.*

Take an unrealistic thought related to sensation-seeking and one related to a problem in life and work through the process to make your thinking more realistic.

Unrealistic Thought About Sensation-Seeking	Feelings After Thinking This	Where Is the Evidence This Is True?

Write a More Realistic Thought:

Unrealistic Thought About a Problem in Your Life	Feelings After Thinking This	Where Is the Evidence This Is True?

Write a More Realistic Thought:

I Was Somewhere Else

People with an addiction to risky behavior and adrenaline rushes often lie to cover up their behavior. They usually do not want to scare loved ones.

Example: JEL tells her partner that she is at the office, but she is diving with sharks.

How have you lied to cover up the risks you take to get a buzz? Below, identify the people you lie to, how you tell lies and the consequences of your lying behavior.

People I Lie To USE NAME CODES	What I Say	Consequences of My Behavior
Example: MSD	*I tell them I need to work overtime at night to cover for my high-stakes poker game.*	*MSD had an emergency and called me on my cell, which I had turned off, and then called work and was told I left at 5. Their trust was broken, and they told me they were taking a two-week break from our relationship.*

I'm not upset that you lied to me, I'm upset that from now on I can't believe you.
~ Friedrich Nietzsche

How does this quote apply in your life, and why?

_____

_____

_____

_____

Curbing Risk-Taking Urges

Many urges prompt you to seek risk. These urges are predicated on the notion that if you find a risk, you will get a rush and feel really good! This may be true, but the rush is temporary and often used to escape life issues and problems. What is permanent are the problems afterward.

In the boxes, identify the urges that trigger your desire to take risks. Next to each, write about how the urge drives your behavior.

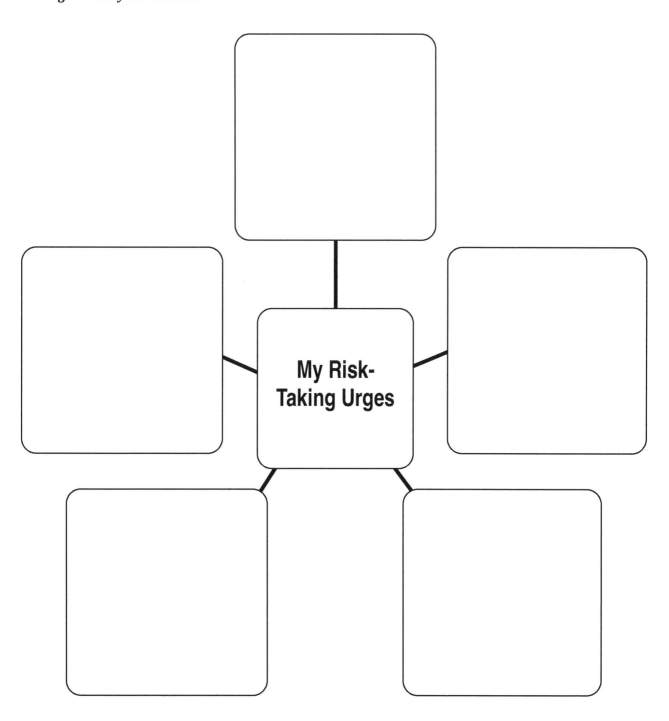

My Risk-Taking Urges

Ways to Be Mindful and Reduce Urges

When you begin to feel the urge to seek sensations, get thrills, or take risks, you need to have a go-to way of being mindful and staying present. How can you reduce the urges associated with risky behavior addiction? Some ways to overcome these urges include practicing yoga, meditating to reduce your irrational thinking, engaging in a compelling hobby, staying mindful of the task at hand, deep breathing, etc.

List your coping mechanisms to resist urges in the hexagons below. Next to each one, identify how well it works or if you want to try it.

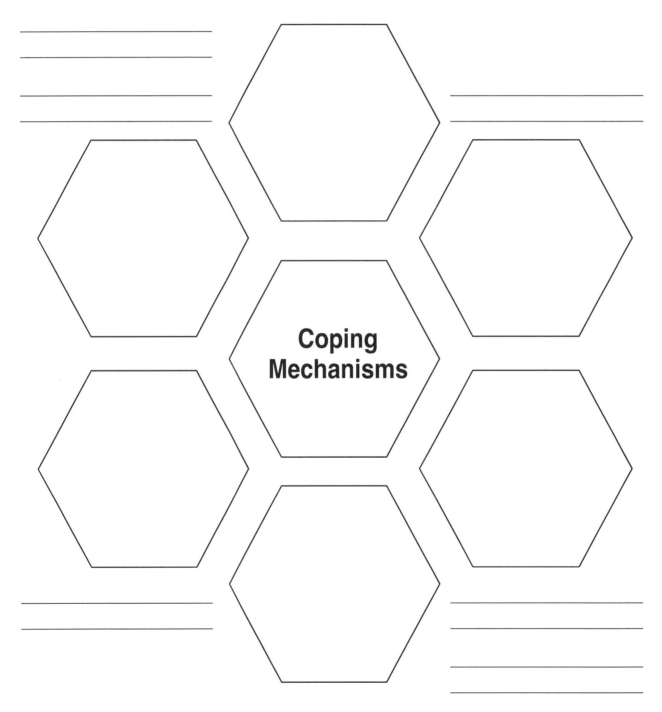

What I Have Lost

Many people with an addiction to risky behavior are so busy chasing the next rush that they forget about all other aspects of their lives. They forget they have a family, a job, friends, etc.

Below, identify what you have lost from the categories in the first column.

Areas of My Life	What I Have Lost
Example: Family	*I was recently divorced because my partner did not like the financial risks I was taking and objected to the fact that I was not checking with her since we pooled our resources.*
Family	
Friends	
Neighbors	
Finances	
Intimate Relationships	
Job/Career	
Other	

The experience of pain or loss can be a formidably motivating force.
~ John C. Maxwell

Please Support Me

Many people addicted to risky behavior do not want to admit their addiction and are unaware of the people who support them. Either way, it is important to identify and strengthen your support network. It is challenging to battle any addiction without support. Reach out to friends and family.

Keep in mind ...
- Supporters are positive people.
- Supporters hold you accountable.
- Supporters can help you overcome your urges to take risks.
- Supporters can direct you to a person or people who can help you.
- Supporters can talk to you about the problems related to your addiction.

Below, list the people in your support network:

My Supporters USE NAME CODE	Relationship to Me	How This Person Supports Me
Example: BNT	*Family Member*	*He is very wise. He listens carefully without judging. He has a lot of connections and can help me find a therapist or financial manager to help me through this.*

Quotes about Mindfulness

Read all three of the quotations below.

#1

Mindfulness helps you go home to the present. And every time you go there and recognize a condition of happiness that you have, happiness comes.
~ Thich Nhat Hanh

#2

Mindfulness can help people of any age. That's because we become what we think.
~ Goldie Hawn

#3

We can have skills training in mindfulness so that we are using our attention to perceive something in the present moment. This perception is not so laden by fears or projections into the future, or old habits, and then I can actually stir loving-kindness or compassion in skills training too, which can be sort of provocative, I found.
~ Sharon Salzberg

Pick a quote that sounds like you and explain why. #_____

_____

_____

Pick one that inspires you to do better and explain how you will do that. #_____

_____

_____

Pick a quote that taught you something and explain what it taught you. #_____

_____

_____

Write your own quote regarding mindfulness.

_____

_____

_____

_____

_____

Adrenaline Need

Name _____

Date _____

Adrenaline Need Assessment
Introduction and Directions

Many people enjoy taking risks because their risk-taking behavior provides a rush of adrenaline. This adrenaline rush usually starts slowly and increases as the behavior and the potential rewards intensify. A little bit of adrenaline can be a good thing! However, when it becomes an addiction, it can have very negative consequences. Adrenaline is a powerful hormone that kicks our bodies into action when we sense danger or prepare for a risky or challenging experience. It's that buzz you get when you're about to ski down a black diamond run or steal a car. Of course, we need this boost in genuinely dangerous situations to react quickly to save ourselves. Left unchecked, it can have serious consequences.

The *Adrenaline Need Assessment* contains 20 statements that describe various consequences of needing an adrenaline rush.

Read each of the statements and decide if the statement describes you. If the statement describes you, place a checkmark in the box in front of the statement. If the statement does not describe you, leave the box in front of the statement empty.

In the following example, the first statement is descriptive of the person completing the assessment, but the second is not:

When it comes to my risk-taking behavior:

☑ I need to take risks to feel excited.

☐ I become irritable when I need to restrict or cut back on risk-taking behaviors.

This is not a test. Since there are no right or wrong answers, do not spend too much time thinking about them. **BE HONEST!**

If you choose, no one else needs to see the results.

(Turn to the next page and begin.)

Adrenaline Need Assessment

Name _____ Date _____

This will only be accurate if you respond honestly. No one else needs to see this if you choose.

When it comes to my risk-taking behavior:

☐ I need to take risks to feel excited.

☐ I become irritable when I need to restrict or cut back on risk-taking behaviors.

☐ I have been unsuccessful in controlling, stopping, or reducing risk-taking behaviors.

☐ I am preoccupied with risk-taking.

☐ I seek ways to get more involved in taking risks.

☐ I use risk-taking to relieve stress.

☐ I engage in risk-taking when I have problems that are difficult to solve.

☐ I like to conceal my risk-taking activity, involvement, or adrenaline rushes.

☐ I jeopardize my relationships, job, or education for the sake of thrills.

☐ I rely on others to help me avoid risk-taking behaviors.

☐ I am dependent on the adrenaline rush received from taking risks.

☐ I often cannot think about anything other than taking more significant risks.

☐ I have noticed a decline in my work/school achievement.

☐ I am no longer interested in social activities unless they involve taking risks.

☐ I take risks to relieve challenging emotions.

☐ I get co-workers to join me in a risk-taking activity to avoid stressful situations.

☐ I can no longer control the intensity of the risks I take.

☐ I feel like risk-taking is dominating my life.

☐ I cannot control my impulses to take risks.

☐ I engage in risk-taking rather than deal with a conflict at home.

Adrenaline Need TOTAL = _____

Go to the next page for scoring assessment results, profile interpretation, and individual description.

Adrenaline Need Assessment

Scoring Directions and Profile Interpretation

The assessment you just completed was created to measure your need for adrenaline.

Count the number of items you checked on the Adrenaline Need Assessment. Put that total on the line marked TOTAL on the assessment at the bottom of the page. Then, transfer your total to this space below:

Adrenaline Need TOTAL = _____

Assessment Profile Interpretation

By checking even ONE statement, you are presently experiencing problems due to an addiction to risky behavior. The more items you checked, the greater your risk of experiencing many issues because of your need for adrenaline.

The HIGHER your score on the *Adrenaline Need Assessment,* **the more of an addiction to risky behavior you are experiencing. Indicate your score on the continuum below.**

---

0 = Low   10 = Moderate   20 = High

How honest were you when you responded to items on the assessment?

_____

_____

Is your score valid?

_____

_____

What is your reaction to your score?

_____

_____

Do you feel you need to do something about your risky behavior addiction issues?

_____

_____

Consequences of Adrenaline

People addicted to risk and adrenaline eventually discover their risk-taking behavior has consequences for themselves and their families. They spend more money than they should, get into legal trouble, have problems with their job performance and availability, and experience physical health issues, anxiety, weight gain, sleeping problems, etc.

Below, identify the consequences of your addiction to risk and adrenaline.

Area Affected	The Consequences	How I Can Limit the Impact on Me and My Family
Example: Finances	*I overspend on my addiction racing cars and motorcycles and I'm behind on my bills.*	*I can find less expensive ways of getting my adrenaline rush – maybe some ways that involve my family, like hiking.*
Finances		
Legal		
Job		
Physical Health		
Mental Health		
Weight Gain or Loss		
Sleep		

What are the three most significant issues you listed above, and what can you do about them?

1. _____

2. _____

3. _____

Leads to Other Addictions

A need for increasing amounts of adrenaline can lead to other addictions too!

Below, identify how you have become addicted to other things.

My Other Addictions	How I Use These Addictions	Other Ways I Could Cope
Example: Exercise	*Exercise gives me the adrenaline rush I need. Unless I exercise once or twice a day, I am miserable.*	*Maybe I can shorten my exercise routine or skip a day and do something else that would be satisfying, like go skating with my family.*
Alcohol/Drugs		
Exercise		
Food		
Gambling		
Gaming		
Love		
Sex		
Shopping		
Technology		
Work		

Need for Urgency

People addicted to risky behavior are often overwhelmed and seem to have a need for urgency, even panic, to get them through the day. This occurs in all aspects of their daily lives. They tend to keep their foot on the accelerator at full speed, convinced that if they slow down, they will miss many opportunities. *For example, in your career, you may work non-stop because you love taking on lots of work and waiting until the last minute to get it done.*

Identify how you keep your foot on the accelerator in the various aspects of your life.

- **My Career**

  _____

  _____

- **My Family Life**

  _____

  _____

- **My Recreational Time**

  _____

  _____

- **My Friendships**

  _____

  _____

- **My Spiritual Life**

  _____

  _____

- **My Risk-Taking Life**

  _____

  _____

- **Other**

  _____

  _____

I am a slow walker, but I never walk back.
~ Abraham Lincoln

I Need More Adrenaline

People addicted to risk-taking and adrenaline often need to feel increasing amounts of adrenaline to feel satisfied. Like someone who abuses substances, they often end their days wondering how their life became so messed up.

Respond to the questions related to your need for risk-taking and adrenaline.

People often vow to take control of their life. Do you? What happens after you pledge this?

_____

_____

When your adrenaline addiction kicks in, how does it provide you with comfort?

_____

_____

When your risk-taking addiction kicks in, how does your personality change?

_____

_____

When your adrenaline addiction kicks in, how are you and your family hurt?

_____

_____

When your risk-taking addiction kicks in, how are you praised for your frantic activity?

_____

_____

When your adrenaline addiction kicks in, do you wear your habit like a badge of honor and stop seeing it as an addiction?

_____

_____

When your risk-taking addiction kicks in, how do you rationalize your behavior?

_____

_____

Are You a Danger to Yourself?

People with an addiction to the adrenaline rush produced by risky behavior often put themselves in dangerous situations to get a buzz. A clear example is the base jumper who keeps jumping from higher levels to get even more of a rush of adrenaline. However, there are other types of dangerous situations:

- The gambler who keeps losing more and more money.
- The person who keeps having affairs and unprotected sex.
- The thief who keeps trying to steal even more massive amounts of money.

Journal about how you put yourself in dangerous situations in the spaces that follow.

My Dangerous Situations	How It Addresses My Risk-Taking and Adrenaline Addiction	How I Could Have Done It More Safely

There are some things you can do to control your body's reaction to a need for adrenaline.
- Slow your breathing or breathe into a paper bag. This can balance the oxygen supply to your body and help you feel calmer and stay in control.
- Exercise can help to distract you. In moderation it is good for you.
- Try yoga or stretching exercises that may also relieve stress and an adrenaline urge.
- Get some fresh air and take a short walk. Notice the beauty of nature.
- Choose and repeat a one or two-word mantra. *(For example: be calm, stay relaxed, breathe deep, etc.)* These mantras will distract from the body's urge for adrenaline.
- Picture a relaxing image. This is another method that may help to reduce the urge.

Seeking the New and Novel

People who are addicted to risky behavior and adrenaline have a unique need for novelty. They need new and different experiences to continue receiving a spike of adrenaline. It soon becomes a compulsive behavior. If you are addicted to risk-taking and adrenaline you might seek new and novel experiences to get thrills. You may look for new and different ways to get those thrills and overdo it with activities such as gambling, seeking romantic/sexual partners, shopping, eating, gaming, exercising, working, technology, or criminal behaviors.

In the circles, identify the novel ways you seek an adrenaline rush. Next to each circle, explain how it is working for you.

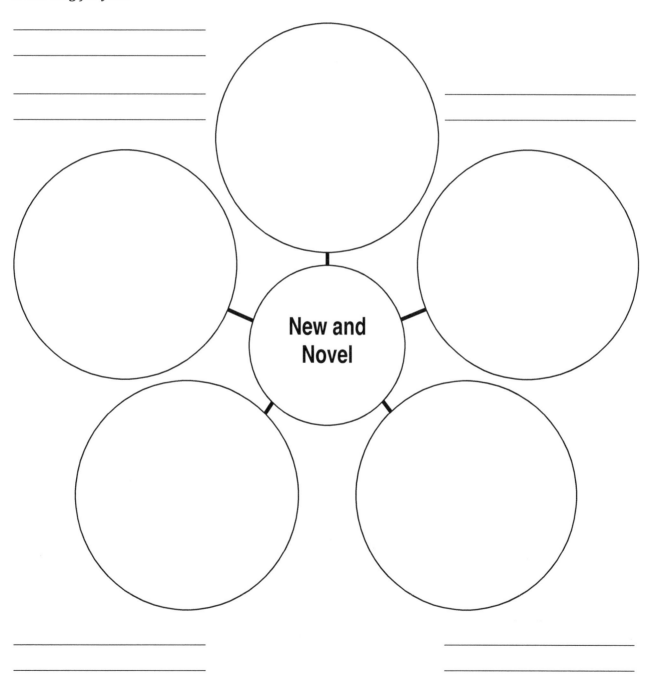

Abandon

When people are addicted to the adrenaline rush from thrill-seeking, they usually abandon activities they enjoyed in the past, such as hobbies, sports, socializing, time with kids and family, etc., because those things do not provide them with a rush. They often continue to engage in thrill-seeking despite the major problems it causes, such as sleep deprivation, relationship struggles, or health concerns.

Explore all of the people and activities you have abandoned.

1. **I have abandoned** _____

_____

2. **I have abandoned** _____

_____

3. **I have abandoned** _____

_____

4. **I have abandoned** _____

_____

5. **I have abandoned** _____

_____

6. **I have abandoned** _____

_____

7. **I have abandoned** _____

_____

Of the seven items above that you have abandoned, circle 2 you can rectify immediately.

1.   2.   3.   4.   5.   6.   7.

Write how you will do that. Later, consider which other ones you can rectify.

Everyday Signs (Page 1)

There are some unique signs that indicate you enjoy and need increasing amounts of adrenaline throughout the day.

Put a check in the box on the signs below that apply to you, and journal about them.

☐ I consume three or more caffeinated drinks daily.

_____

_____

☐ I am guilty of frequent offensive driving behavior (speeding, tailgating, road rage, etc.).

_____

_____

☐ I constantly cancel events at home to schedule my risky activities.

_____

_____

☐ I enjoy meetings and events with little down-time in between.

_____

_____

☐ I am always on-the-go!

_____

_____

☐ I frequently cause (and enjoy) drama between me and others.

_____

_____

Everyday Signs (Page 2)

There are some unique signs that indicate you enjoy and need increasing amounts of adrenaline throughout the day.

Put a check in the box on the signs below that apply to you, and journal about them.

☐ **I knowingly put myself into stressful situations.**

_____

_____

☐ **I love having the image of a risk-taker.**

_____

_____

☐ **I get very little sleep because there are too many things to do.**

_____

_____

Now, in the spaces that follow, identify a few of your own:

I _____

_____

I _____

_____

I _____

_____

I _____

_____

My Whole Life

For people with an addiction to risky behavior and adrenaline, life tends to revolve around the addiction. An addiction can determine who you hang out with, whether you still maintain your relationships or commitments, when you have time for family, how you perform at your job, etc.

In each of the hexagons below, explore ways in which your addiction affects your whole life. Use the space beside them to contemplate what you can do about it.

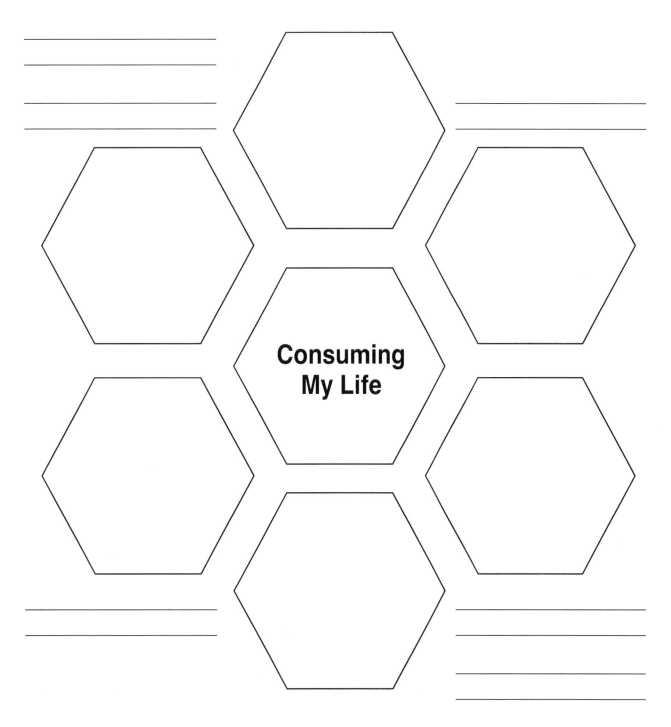

Tremendous Amounts of Stress

People who spend the majority of their time thinking about, planning for, and engaging in high-risk activities often find themselves under tremendous amounts of stress and experiencing unhappiness created by poor performance at work, problems at home, and issues with their family relationships and friendships.

Write, doodle, or draw the ways your performance may be decreasing. If one of the areas listed below is not being affected, feel free to change the title of the box. On the bottom half of each section, write, doodle, or draw the ways you can do something about it!

Family Members – Decreasing	Intimate Relationships – Decreasing
What I Can Do About It:	What I Can Do About It:
My Job – Decreasing	My Friendships – Decreasing
What I Can Do About It:	What I Can Do About It:

Believe you can and you're halfway there.
~ Theodore Roosevelt

Family Effects

An addiction to risk and adrenaline can, and usually does, affect all aspects of your life. It can also have a devastatingly negative effect on every member of your family. It is vital to take care of them and not let this addiction take over your life, or theirs.

How I Gave in to My Addiction	How It Affected My Family	How I Can Change My Ways to Make Sure It Never Happens Again
Example: I traded stocks online.	I spent so much money that we needed to move from our home.	I will consult a financial planner with my partner so we're on the same page about how we're investing.

The bond that links your true family is not one of blood,
but of respect and joy in each other's life.
~ Richard Bach

Describe how the above quotation is true, or untrue, of your family?

_____

_____

_____

_____

Your Own Needs

People struggling with an addiction to risky behavior might notice how they neglect their own needs to serve their addiction and get a rush. They might compromise by eating unhealthy foods, neglecting sleep, working too long, avoiding exercise or a doctor's visit, or behaving unsafely. When people neglect their personal needs, they will eventually see the consequences of their behavior.

Below, identify how you are neglecting your own needs and how you can start to take better care of yourself.

How I Am Neglecting My Needs	The Adrenaline Rush I Seek Instead	How I Can Do a Better Job Taking Care of My Needs
Example: I exercise compulsively. Then I have no time left to have fun and enjoy my family.	*I love the feeling that comes during and right after I exercise. I like looking in the mirror at the results.*	*I need to make a reasonable exercise schedule, not every day for hours, but one that still keeps me buff and strong.*

© 2023 WHOLE PERSON ASSOCIATES, 101 WEST 2ND STREET, SUITE 203, DULUTH MN 55802 • 800-247-6789 • WHOLEPERSON.COM

Putting Myself in Danger

Adrenaline junkies often put themselves into dangerous situations in various ways. These situations can be financially, physically, mentally, socially, sexually, and occupationally dangerous, leading the person to become overly stressed and to destroy valuable relationships.

Below, explore how you put yourself in dangerous situations.

The Situation	How I Put Myself In Danger	What I Feel
Example: I engage in street racing every night.	*I race other drivers on an open road.*	*I feel exhilarated, even though I could crash and die at any moment.*

A huge adrenaline rush is usually followed by a pretty low point.
~ Bode Miller

Meditation Tip: The next time you feel the need for adrenaline, try meditation. Meditation has been shown to improve your mental outlook, increase happiness, enhance self-control, and reduce adrenaline. There are many different types of meditation, but the main benefit is relaxation. Most meditation types will help you relax and get you on the right track if you are consistent with your practice. Even 15 minutes a day before bed or during an adrenaline urge will provide great benefits. How can you begin to incorporate meditation into your daily routine?

Building a Tolerance

People often build a tolerance to their addiction to risky behavior and adrenaline. As addicts continue to take risks, they require increasingly intense and frequent thrills to experience the same adrenaline rush.

In the boxes on the left, list the risky behaviors you use most often. On the lines to the right, describe how you have built a tolerance.

Example: Unprotected Sex ⟶ *I started by having unprotected sex once in while with people I knew. Eventually I found myself having sex with multiple strangers each week.*

Quotes about Addiction to Adrenaline

Read all three of the quotations below.

#1

I'm up for challenges. I'm up for being outside the box, making
tough decisions and challenges... And I'm a little bit of an adrenaline junkie.
~ Becky Hammon

#2

Acceptance of what has happened is the first step to overcoming
the consequences of any misfortune.
~ William James

#3

I am sufficiently wary of dangerous situations,
but I'm not scared of having a go.
~ Catherine Martin

Pick a quote that sounds like you and explain why. #_____

_____

_____

Pick one that inspires you to do better and explain how you will do that. #_____

_____

_____

Pick a quote that taught you something and explain what it taught you. #_____

_____

_____

Write your own quote regarding adrenaline addiction behaviors.

_____

_____

_____

_____

_____

_____

_____

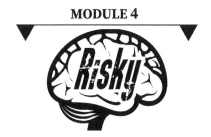

Risk-Taking Personality

Name _____

Date _____

Risk-Taking Personality Assessment
Introduction and Directions

People who are addicted to risky behavior often display it in their personality. They will do anything to avoid boredom and feel an adrenaline rush. One or two of these traits may not necessarily be a problem, but too many can lead to an addiction to risky behavior. Awareness of these traits can be the starting point of recovery.

The *Risk-Taking Personality Assessment* contains 20 statements that define risk-taking personality traits. This assessment can help you gauge the extent to which risk-taking is a problem in your life.

Read each of the statements and decide if they describe you. If the statement describes you, circle the number in the YES column next to that item. If the statement does not describe you, circle the number in the NO column next to that item.

In the following example, the circled 1 indicates that the person completing this assessment does not believe that the statement describes them:

	YES	NO
I cannot control my impulses	2	1
I take many death-defying risks	2	1

This is not a test. Since there are no right or wrong answers, do not spend too much time thinking about them. **BE HONEST!**

If you choose, no one else needs to see the results.

(Turn to the next page and begin.)

Risk-Taking Personality Assessment

Name _____ Date _____

This will only be accurate if you respond honestly. No one else needs to see this if you choose.

	YES	NO
I cannot control my impulses	2	1
I take many death-defying risks	2	1
I seek constant change	2	1
I often engage in unplanned behavior	2	1
I detest predictability	2	1
I constantly seek new and novel situations	2	1
I take risks that negatively affect my life	2	1
I tend to be extremely impulsive	2	1
I have mood swings	2	1
I tend to make decisions too quickly	2	1
I love intense situations	2	1
I often lack self-control	2	1
I am attracted to any type of thrill	2	1
I am sad when I am not taking extreme risks	2	1
I need stimulating expriences	2	1
I hate being bored with mundane things	2	1
I crave thrills in life	2	1
I will put my life in danger for a "buzz"	2	1
I engage in risks to relieve stress	2	1
I become bored very easily	2	1

Risk-Taking Personality TOTAL = _____

Go to the next page for scoring assessment results, profile interpretation, and individual description.

Risk-Taking Personality Assessment

Scoring Directions and Profile Interpretation

The assessment you just completed is designed to measure the extent of your risk-taking personality.

Add the numbers you circled on the Risk-Taking Personality Assessment. Put the total on the line marked TOTAL at the end of the section on the assessment. Then, transfer your total to this space below:

Risk-Taking Personality TOTAL = _____

Assessment Profile Interpretation

Even ONE answer from the YES column means you might be at risk for developing an addiction to risky behavior. The more answers from the YES column you circled, the greater the possibility you have of experiencing a problem with your risky behavior.

This assessment measures how much of a risk-taking personality you have. The HIGHER your score on the *Risk-Taking Personality Assessment,* the more you need to take care of yourself and be careful of the types of risks you are taking.

20 = Low	30 = Moderate	40 = High

Take calculated risks. That is quite different from being rash.
~ General George Patton

How does this quotation apply to you?

_____

_____

_____

_____

I'm Bored!

People addicted to risky behavior need their fix. This need is especially noticeable when they are bored. During these times of boredom, addicts are most vulnerable to their addiction. They need to identify non-risk-taking activities (gardening, yoga, watching movies, etc.) to cut through the boredom.

Below, write about the times you tend to get bored throughout the week. What is going on? How could non-risk activities overcome your boredom?

Days of the Week	Where Am I? What is Going On?	How I Could Have Managed My Boredom in a Non-Risk-Taking Manner
Example: Sunday	*I am home. My family members are all doing their own thing. Cleaning, homework, watching TV, playing video games.*	*I could say, how about if I help you finish what you need to do, and then we go to the new movie and dinner afterwards?*
Sunday		
Monday		
Tuesday		
Wednesday		
Thursday		
Friday		
Saturday		

It is important to remember these activities may not provide the same type of rush as risky behavior. Still, they will help keep you busy and help reduce the need for the adrenaline rush.

Thoughts in My Head

Exploring negative thoughts that come along with your risk-taking behavior is important. These thoughts might include "I am a loser." or "There's more to life than this!" or "All that matters is my next thrill."

Below, identify the thoughts that go through your head before and during risk-taking behaviors. Then identify more realistic thoughts you can tell yourself to counteract the negative thoughts.

Thoughts That Go Through My Head	More Realistic Thoughts
Example: Rock climbing is all there is in life that I love.	*Rock climbing is only one aspect of my life. I can also spend time hiking with my kids and planning a date with my spouse.*

The language we use is extremely powerful. It is the frame through which we perceive and describe ourselves and our picture of the world.
~ Iben Dissing Sandahl

My Impulse Control

People with an addiction often lack impulse control. On the line under each example, place an X on the continuum that indicates your involvement with that particular behavior. Write why you rated yourself that way on the dotted line below each one. **BE HONEST!**

I act on the spur of the moment.

0 (Not Much)   5 (A Little)   10 (A Great Deal)

I do things that I regret later.

0 (Not Much)   5 (A Little)   10 (A Great Deal)

I give in to the risky behavior rush.

0 (Not Much)   5 (A Little)   10 (A Great Deal)

I don't pause and think before I act.

0 (Not Much)   5 (A Little)   10 (A Great Deal)

I do things impulsively.

0 (Not Much)   5 (A Little)   10 (A Great Deal)

The higher your score on each scale above, the more of a problem you have with an addiction to risky behavior. Areas where you scored lower suggest you are not experiencing many aspects of an addiction to risky behavior in those areas.

How much will your life change positively if you overcome your addiction?

0 (Not Much)   5 (A Little)   10 (A Great Deal)

Do you want to change your current risk-taking habits?

0 (Not Much)   5 (A Little)   10 (A Great Deal)

Triggers of My Boredom

People with a risk-taking personality can be helped by recognizing the triggers that precede their urge for adrenaline. These triggers can include people, places, memories, feelings, advertisements, scenes from a book, television, the news, movies, etc.

Reflect on the times you have become bored. Below, discuss the psychological and physical triggers you experience before boredom sets in. USE NAME CODES.

Triggers USE NAME CODES	When I Was Bored	How It Affected Me
Example: People	*I had to stay at home during the pandemic with my family.*	*I tried to stay busy with the family, but it was difficult. Everyone was bored and arguing. We finally started playing games, and that helped.*
People		
Memories		
Feelings		
Ads		
Scenes from a Book, TV, or Movie		
News		
Other		

Boredom is just the reverse side of fascination: both depend on being outside rather than inside a situation, and one leads to the other.
~ Arthur Schopenhauer

Preventing Risk-Taking Behavior

Boredom often leads to risk-taking behavior. If you get bored easily, you can benefit from identifying ways to prevent boredom before it occurs. Think about preventative measures, and journal about how you can integrate them into your daily routine.

Below, note the time, place, and what is happening before you get bored.

Time and Place I Get Bored	What is Occurring?	How I Know If I'm Getting Bored	How I Can Prevent Boredom
Example: Saturday evenings, in my house.	*I have finished dinner and don't have anything to do.*	*I start walking around my house, looking out the windows.*	*Arrange a game night with friends each Saturday after dinner.*

As you reflect on your answers, which prevention strategy do you think will be most effective? Why?

_____

_____

_____

When you pay attention to boredom it gets unbelievably interesting.
~ Jon Kabat-Zinn

I Get Bored!

Think about how you seek risky behavior when you are bored.

Respond to the following sentence starters to learn more about yourself and your behavior.

When I am bored, I ...

_____

_____

_____

When I am bored, my first thoughts are to ...

_____

_____

_____

When I am bored, I wish ...

_____

_____

_____

When I am bored, I impulsively ...

_____

_____

_____

When I am bored, I engage in some of these risk-taking behaviors ...

_____

_____

_____

When I am bored, I can engage in some of these non-risk-taking behaviors ...

_____

_____

_____

My Life is Boring

Because the tendency to get bored is foundational to a risk-taking personality, it is crucial to identify why you feel your life is boring. Is your work and life in general monotonous? Are you ready for something or someone new? Are you unable to find fun things to do?

In the squares below, identify the things that you find boring. Then, outside of each, write about why you find that aspect of your life boring and how you can be creative and make it less boring!

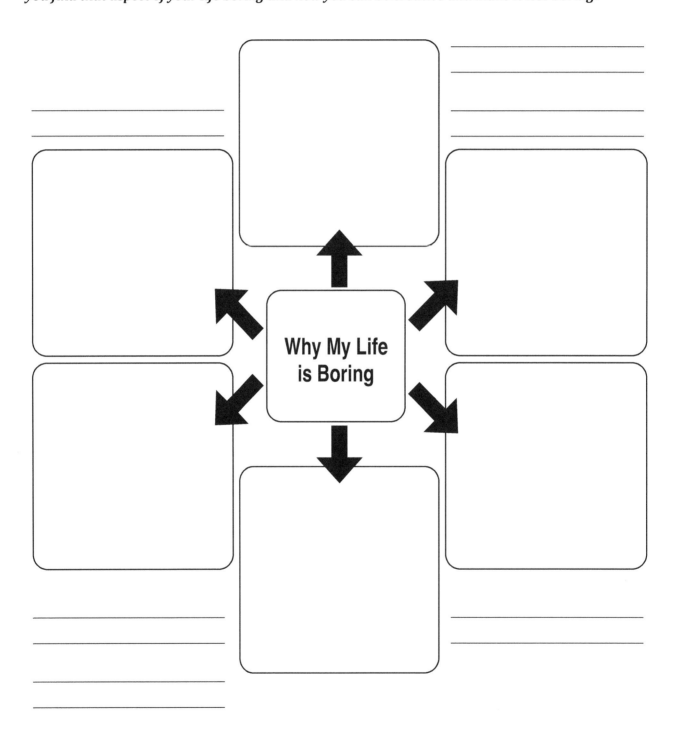

Motivation in My Personal Life

By staying motivated and engaged in non-risk-taking activities, people addicted to risky behavior can reduce the impact of their urges. Focusing on personal goals can help lessen the pull of adrenaline.

Below, explore your personal goals (family, relationships, friends, etc.).

Where I want to be and what I want to be doing in my personal life five years from now:

_____

_____

_____

_____

_____

_____

_____

Think about the goals you can now set for getting to where you want to be in 5 years.

Goal #1: _____

Goal #2: _____

Goal #3: _____

Goal #4: _____

Goal #5: _____

Now describe 5 of the non-risk-taking tasks you need to complete that will help you meet the above goals.

1. _____

2. _____

3. _____

4. _____

5. _____

Motivation in My Professional Life

In the previous exercise, you explored personal goals. Now take a look at your professional goals. By staying motivated and engaged in non-risk-taking activities, people addicted to risky behavior can reduce the impact of their urges. Focusing on professional goals can help lessen the pull of adrenaline.

Below, explore your professional goals (career, education, work changes).

Where I want to be and what I want to be doing in my professional life five years from now:

_____

_____

_____

_____

_____

_____

_____

Think about the goals you can now set for getting to where you want to be in 5 years.

Goal #1: _____

Goal #2: _____

Goal #3: _____

Goal #4: _____

Goal #5: _____

Now describe 5 of the non-risk-taking tasks you need to complete that will help you meet the above goals.

1. _____

2. _____

3. _____

4. _____

5. _____

Are You Restless?

Boredom can force unpleasant restlessness in people, and it often triggers an active search for ways out of the boredom mindset. Restlessness can often be diminished by identifying alternative activities, hobbies, leisure interests, friends, or work.

Inside each box below, identify some of the alternative activities you can engage in to overcome your general sense of restlessness.

Family activities and how they will help relieve my restlessness.

Leisure activities and how they will help relieve my restlessness.

Work activities and how they will help relieve my restlessness.

Spiritual or religious activities and how they will help relieve my restlessness.

Ways to Replace Boredom

Boredom can be avoided by focusing on non-risk activities. These activities can calm the mind so that it is not as reactive to urges for risk and adrenaline.

Read each prompt, then journal about ways you will replace boredom.

**Spend some time in quiet contemplation considering what's important to you.
What comes to mind?**

What are creative projects you could begin to replace boredom?

How can you be more involved with family and friends?

Boredom or discontent is useful to me when I acknowledge it and see clearly
my assumption that there's something else I would rather be doing.
~ Hugh Prather

Adrenaline Quote

Adrenaline really numbs out all pain.
~ Alissa White-Gluz

What does the above quote mean to you?

_____

_____

_____

How do your adrenaline rushes numb your pain?

_____

_____

_____

What type of pain are you in (emotional, physical, financial, etc.)?

_____

_____

_____

How can you address the pain so you do not need to numb it?

_____

_____

_____

Are there other ways to reduce your pain without relying on ever-increasing amounts of adrenaline?

_____

_____

_____

Are you willing to try ways to reduce your pain without relying on ever-increasing amounts of adrenaline? If yes, why? If no, why not?

_____

_____

_____

Healthy Ways to Deal with Boredom

When people are bored, they can switch to creative, healthy ways of coping rather than turning to unhealthy or risky ways of dealing with this issue.

Below, identify some healthy, positive ways you can overcome boredom.

Healthy Ways I've Tried to Overcome Boredom	How It Helped	The Effects It Will Have on My Life
Example: I decided to try to learn to speak Spanish so I could talk with my neighbor, who does not speak English.	*I started looking forward to the challenge of learning and mastering a new language.*	*I will be able to speak to her and some other neighbors who speak only Spanish. It will make me feel outstanding!*

Why is boredom difficult for you to deal with when there are many creative and wonderful things to do?

_____

_____

_____

_____

Finding My Non-Risk Purpose

People sometimes become so wrapped up in their risky behavior in order to feel an adrenaline rush that they never grow into their real purpose in life. They mistakenly believe that their adrenaline rushes are their purpose.

Answer the following questions to find your real purpose in life. Exclude all risk-taking behaviors.

Some things I love to do are ...

_____

_____

Some things I do well are ...

_____

_____

The qualities I enjoy expressing are ...

_____

_____

What the community needs from me is ...

_____

_____

My heart tells me to ...

_____

_____

My ideal life is when ...

_____

_____

_____

I care about _____ so much.

It deeply moves me because _____

_____

The greatest joy in life is when I am _____

When I am doing this I am _____

Connection Between Thoughts and Emotions

Your thoughts can dramatically affect the emotions you feel. Thoughts provide fuel for boredom and impulsivity. When you feel bored, the little voice in your head might say you need to find a new sensation, promoting the drive toward impulsivity.

When you practice mindfulness, you will no longer see thoughts as problems to deal with. Instead, you can see that thoughts are not solid objects, and you can begin to let go of them.

Give an example of how your recent thoughts have negatively influenced your drive toward risk-taking behavior.

_____

_____

_____

_____

Sometimes it can be helpful to become more mindful by labeling your thoughts. Try this activity below:

1. Sit in a comfortable, upright position. Keep your feet on the floor as you do this activity.
2. Bring awareness to your breath. Spend about five minutes mindfully counting your breaths.
3. From time to time, you will notice that your attention is moving from your breath to random thoughts. Each time you notice this, say silently to yourself, "Thinking." Bring awareness back to your breath. Try not to judge yourself negatively as you do this.
4. As your mind wanders, label each thought as "Thinking" and return to your breath.

How did you feel during the activity and afterward?

_____

_____

_____

_____

Explain why it was easy or difficult.

_____

_____

_____

_____

Bored at Work

Many people who are bored at work do not engage in risky behaviors on purpose. However, they do find ways to make work an adrenaline rush.

Explore ways you attempt to get an adrenaline rush at work. First, respond to the statements provided, then add some of your own below.

Work Activities	When I Do This	How It Makes Me feel
I am always late, and then I must rush and run into the building to get there on time.		
I am on personal e-mail and social media at work even though I might get fired.		
I book a tight schedule in order to run from meeting to meeting without stopping.		
I leave projects undone until the last moment, then I work frantically to get them done.		
I set unrealistic time frames to accomplish my work, then I need to rush.		
I take on too much work, then I stay at work all night to get it done.		
I stay busy every minute of the workday without taking lunch or breaks.		
Other:		
Other:		

Quotes about Boredom

Read all three of the quotations below.

#1

Are you bored with life? Then throw yourself into some work you believe in
with all your heart, live for it, die for it, and you will find happiness
that you had thought could never be yours.
~ Dale Carnegie

#2

You'll find boredom where there is the absence of a good idea.
~ Earl Nightingale

#3

Boredom is the root of all evil - the despairing refusal to be oneself.
~ Soren Kierkegaard

Pick a quote that sounds like you and explain why. #_____

_____

_____

Pick one that inspires you to do better and explain how you will do that. #_____

_____

_____

Pick a quote that taught you something and explain what it taught you. #_____

_____

_____

Write your own quote regarding boredom.

_____

_____

_____

_____

_____

_____

_____

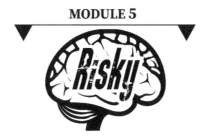

Risk Prevention

Name _____

Date _____

Risk Prevention Assessment
Introduction and Directions

There is a direct correlation between adrenaline and risk. When people have an addiction to risky behavior, the best way to deal with it is to calm themselves and reduce the urge to take that risk. This can be done through prevention. A wide variety of prevention techniques can be utilized to minimize risky behavior urges. It can be helpful for people to look back on their lives, experiences, and actions to find the source of their need for risky behavior and then learn tools and techniques for calming themselves. Many strategies are available for people to overcome a risky behavior addiction.

This assessment is designed to help you understand how effective you are, or are not, in preventing and coping with risky behavior urges.

Read each statement carefully. Circle the number of the response that describes you.
3 = True   2 = Somewhat True   1 = Not True

In the following example, the circled 2 indicates that the statement is Somewhat True for the person completing the scale:

	TRUE	SOMEWHAT TRUE	NOT TRUE
In dealing with my risky behavior urges ...			
I have excellent coping skills.	3	(2)	1
I know how to reduce my stress when I need to.	3	(2)	1

This is not a test. Since there are no right or wrong answers, do not spend too much time thinking about them. **BE HONEST!**

If you choose, no one else needs to see the results.

(Turn to the next page and begin.)

Risk Prevention Assessment

Name _____ Date _____

This will only be accurate if you respond honestly. No one else needs to see this if you choose.

	TRUE	SOMEWHAT TRUE	NOT TRUE
In dealing with my risky behavior urges ...			
I have excellent coping skills	3	2	1
I know how to reduce my stress when I need to	3	2	1
I do not act impulsively	3	2	1
I can confront my mistaken beliefs	3	2	1
I have a support system to help manage my urges	3	2	1
I am assertive when I need to be	3	2	1
I can easily monitor and correct my self-talk	3	2	1
I use visualizations to help reduce stress and anxiety	3	2	1
I use relaxation techniques to relax my body	3	2	1
I take care of myself and my personal needs	3	2	1
I am comfortable saying "no" when I need to	3	2	1
I do not need approval from others	3	2	1
I do not try to live up to the expectations of others	3	2	1
I manage my stress well	3	2	1
I exercise two times a week for an hour to feel better	3	2	1
I rarely try to control things I cannot control	3	2	1
I try to nurture myself when I feel bored	3	2	1
I work on maintaining my self-esteem	3	2	1
I have meaning and purpose in my life	3	2	1
I look to my religious and spiritual beliefs	3	2	1

Risk Prevention TOTAL = _____

Go to the next page for scoring assessment results, profile interpretation, and individual description.

Risk Prevention Assessment

Scoring Directions and Profile Interpretation

Add the numbers you circled on the Risk Prevention Assessment and write that score on the line marked TOTAL on that page. Then transfer that total to the space below:

Risk Prevention TOTAL = _____

Assessment Profile Interpretation

Place an X on the continuum line to represent your score.

20 = Low	33	40 = Moderate	46	60 = High

Scores from 20 to 33 are LOW and suggest that you are not doing a great job of preventing and coping with risky behavior urges.

Scores from 34 to 46 are MODERATE and suggest that you are doing a pretty good job of preventing and coping with risky behavior urges.

Scores from 47 to 60 are HIGH and suggest that you are doing a great job of preventing and coping with risky behavior urges.

What is your reaction to your score?

_____

_____

_____

Look at the statements again on the assessment. How will you commit to preventing risky behavior?

_____

_____

_____

No More Stimulants

Stimulants will exacerbate your addiction to risky behavior and cause further problems. To overcome your addiction, you need to avoid foods that contain stimulating chemicals, including dextroamphetamine (Dexedrine, Dextrostat, ProCentra), lisdexamfetamine (Vyvanse), methylphenidate (Concerta, Daytrana, Methylin, Ritalin), and the combination of amphetamine and dextroamphetamine, etc. Some of these products may contain stimulants: coffee, energy bars, energy drinks, sodas, green and black tea, dark chocolate, espresso, anything with chocolate.

If you are serious about achieving a new normal regarding your risky behavior addiction, the above are chemicals that stimulate the adrenaline rush and should be eliminated from your diet completely.

Take some time to research the ingredients you usually ingest. Do the products you often eat, drink, or smoke include any of the above ingredients? Some brands may and some may not. It's worth taking the time to investigate.

Name/Brand of Foods or Drinks I Often Ingest	Does It Have Any of the Stimulants? What Are They?	If It Has a Stimulant, Will You Continue to Consume It? Why?	If It Has a Stimulant, Will You Stop Consuming It? Why?

Urges Reduced

People addicted to risky behavior need quick tools and techniques that help them avoid or reduce addictive urges as they occur. Rather than engaging in thrill-seeking behavior, find other ways to minimize stress and reduce urges.

List some of your favorite ways of minimizing stress, which can then reduce risky behavior urges.

Ways to Minimize Stress and Reduce Urges	The Results When I Tried It in The Past	How I Will Give This a Try Again
Example: Be mindful and stay in the present	*I couldn't relax and ended up making more risky trades.*	*Set a timer and move into a guided mindfulness meditation.*
Take a Break or Rest		
Talk With a Supportive Person You Trust		
Exercise		
Do Something Fun		
Breathe Deeply		
Meditate		
Be Mindful and Stay in the Present		
Get More and Better Sleep		
Go For a Walk, Hike, or Bike Ride		
Manage Your Time		
Other		

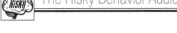

Busy All the Time

People addicted to risky behavior stay busy most of the time. When they are active, they keep the adrenaline flowing throughout their body. They exhibit many of the tendencies below.

Read each statement. If it applies to you, place a checkmark before the item. Then journal about how it applies to you.

☐ I have a strong compulsion to be "doing something" while I am home.

_____

_____

☐ I am obsessed with thoughts about something that remains to be done.

_____

_____

☐ I feel guilty when I am resting or napping rather than doing something.

_____

_____

☐ I fidget, become restless, pace, or cannot concentrate for very long if I'm not doing something constructive.

_____

_____

☐ I often become irritable or aggravated when not engaging in risky behavior.

_____

_____

☐ Whenever I stop an activity, I have a vague feeling of depression.

_____

_____

☐ Even when I am on vacation, I have a strong compulsion to be "doing something meaningful."

_____

_____

Consider Volunteering

To Volunteer: To give of yourself in service to a cause. It is about freely giving your time to help an organization, your community, or an individual.

Going out and volunteering sounds simple, but many people
don't volunteer because they don't know where to start.
~ Mark Foster

Here is a way to start! Below, identify some of the places you might volunteer. This will help you to stop focusing on yourself and to focus on others.

Places I Could Volunteer	What I Could Do	How It Would Be Good for Me
Example: A local animal shelter	*I could take animals for walks.*	*It would give me something to look forward to. It would not be an adrenaline rush, but I think I would feel terrific.*

Share and discuss the ideas listed above with others until you find the perfect place for you to volunteer.

Overall Well-Being

A risky behavior addiction can be significantly reduced by taking care of your daily needs.

Below, identify how your lifestyle is contributing to your risky behavior addiction.

Lifestyle Factors	My Adrenaline Choices	How I Enhanced My Well-Being	How I Can Cope Better
Example: Food Choices	*I drink a lot of coffee.*	*I stopped drinking coffee to reduce adrenaline rushes. I switched to water and decaf tea.*	*Avoid coffee shops and stay away from the coffee machine at work. Bring my water bottle.*
Food Choices			
Exercise			
Sleep			
Relaxation			
Support System			
Spirituality			
Other			

Well-being is attained by little and little, and nevertheless is no little thing itself.
~ Zeno of Citium

How I See Me

People with a risky behavior addiction often see themselves in very different ways. They often see a risk-taking self and a non-risk-taking self. Although these pictures are distinct, the risk-taking self often takes over.

Imagine there are two "mirrors" below.

Pretend you are looking in the "Risk-Taking-Me" mirror and create a list of words in the top box that describe you as a risk-taker. Then draw an example in the mirror below.

Now, move to the "Non-Risk-Taking-Me" mirror on the right and create a list of words in the top box that describe you as a non-risk-taker. Draw an example in the mirror below.

Risk-Taking-Me	Non-Risk-Taking-Me
Image of Risk-Taking-Me	**Image of Non-Risk-Taking-Me**

Which of the two mirrors (risk-taking or non-risk-taking) most accurately describes you? Why?

_____

_____

_____

Your Support System

Everyone needs a support system, especially people with addictions. Let your trusted family members, friends, co-workers, and anyone else who can support you know that you are trying to overcome an addiction. They can encourage your efforts and help keep you accountable.

In the boxes below, list your primary support system and how they can support you.

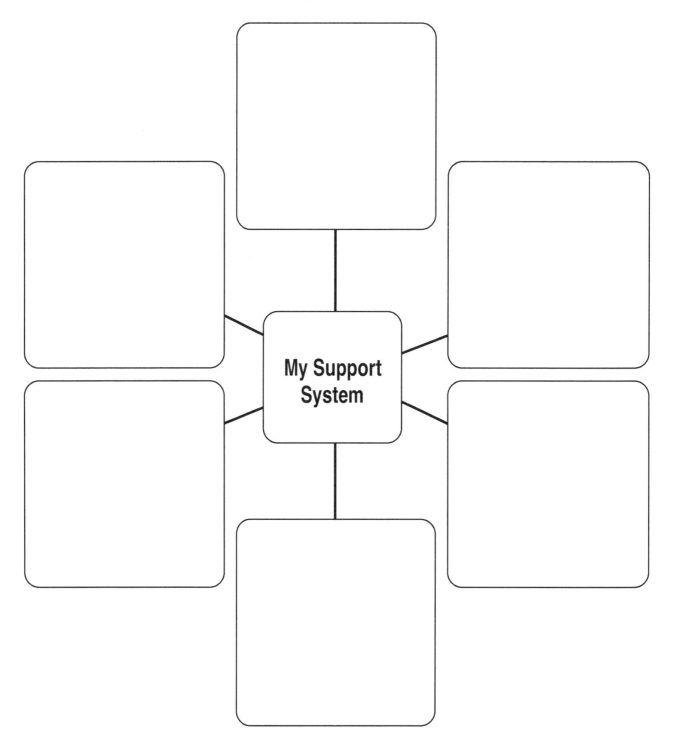

Peer Pressure to Take Risks

Peer pressure does not only occur in the teen years. Adults also receive social pressure from friends, family, or strangers to engage with them in risky or dangerous behavior.

Identify your social pressure situations in the hexagons below:

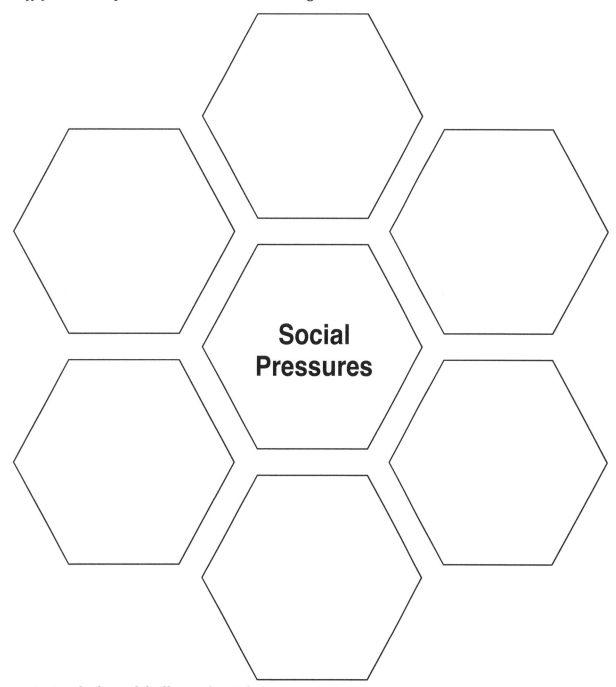

Social Pressures

To minimize the harmful effects of social pressure ...
- **Engage in activities that are not risk-oriented.**
- **Stay away from friends who pressure you to participate in addictive behaviors.**
- **Slow down, calm yourself, relax, and watch what you eat and drink.**

I Tried to Stop

People who try to stop seeking adrenaline rushes through risky behavior tend to experience withdrawal symptoms. Like substance abusers, they cannot stop engaging in risky behavior without experiencing some of the symptoms listed below.

For each withdrawal symptom, explain how you were affected when trying to stop taking risks.

Withdrawal Symptoms	How Long I Stopped Risky Behaviors	How I Was Affected By the Symptom
Example: Lethargy	*In June for one week.*	*I just wanted to lie around the house.*
Lethargy		
Sadness		
Agitation and Irritability		
Restlessness		
Impatience		
Poor Sleep		
Mood Swings		
Restless Leg Syndrome		
Anxiety		
Other		

Avoiding

Start to avoid risky behavior and find healthy ways to have fun. You can avoid risky experiences that make it harder for you to overcome your addiction. Avoid skydiving, gambling, skiing, surfing, rock climbing, betting, practicing unsafe sex, etc. By enjoying doing other things, you will release yourself from your urges to seek adrenaline rushes.

List your top five possibilities for healthy fun in the circles below.

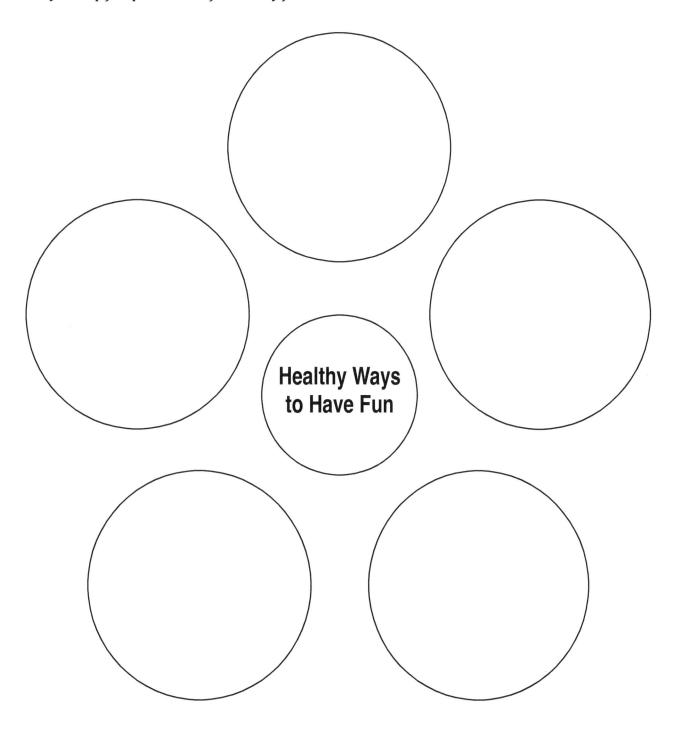

General Adrenaline Factors

People with risky behavior addiction often have some general things they do during the day to keep the adrenaline pumping until they engage in their risk-taking behavior.

Place a checkmark in front of examples that apply to you. Journal about why you do it and how you plan to stop.

☐ I drink coffee, colas, or other caffeine to get going.

_____

_____

☐ I eat sugar to keep the rush alive.

_____

_____

☐ I tend to be impatient when others are not doing what I want as fast as I would like.

_____

_____

☐ I tend to overpromise on my commitments and then struggle to finish.

_____

_____

☐ I rush to get projects done at the last minute.

_____

_____

☐ I arrive at work rushed.

_____

_____

☐ I tend to run late or arrive just in time.

_____

_____

☐ I often drive at least 10 miles per hour over the speed limit.

_____

_____

☐ I look for a challenge, and I love pushing myself to achieve it.

_____

_____

Signs that my adrenaline rushes are harming me and my relationships:

_____

_____

Getting Away

Addictions help people temporarily escape life issues, sometimes at a dangerous cost. The problem with this approach is that the issues are still there after engaging in risky behavior.

Write about, draw, or doodle representations of what you are escaping from when you engage in risky behavior.

I Am Trying to Escape from or Avoid …	I Am Trying to Escape from or Avoid …
I Am Trying to Escape from or Avoid …	**I Am Trying to Escape from or Avoid …**

Think you're escaping and run into yourself.
Longest way round is the shortest way home.
~ James Joyce

Dealing with Risk-Taking Urges

One of the most critical aspects of risk prevention is dealing effectively with risk-taking urges. These urges can hit at any time, and you need to be prepared when you feel them coming on.

The next time you are being confronted by an urge for risky behavior, try the following techniques. Journal about how you think they will work for you and why you feel that way.

Stop isolating yourself. Be with other people, whether in your support network or not. Who are the people with whom you want to start spending more time?

_____

_____

Try to postpone the risk-taking urge. Think of something else, distract yourself, tell yourself to wait a few minutes and see if the urge passes. How has this worked for you in the past?

_____

_____

Visualize the worst-case scenario. Try picturing what will happen if you give in to your urges to take unhealthy risks. What typically happens when you give in?

_____

_____

Examine the after-effects. Think about how you'll feel when you are done, and you've disappointed yourself and your family again. Has this happened to you? Explain.

_____

_____

Distract yourself when you get an urge. Immediately, engage in another activity like listening to music, watching a movie, or reading a great book. What works for you?

_____

_____

Relax. Practice relaxation exercises such as deep breathing, going for a walk, qi gong, meditation, or gardening.

_____

_____

Adrenaline Rushes

People with an addiction to risky behavior always seek adrenaline rushes.

On the line under each of the ways you seek rushes, place an X on the continuum indicating how much you relate to each statement. On the dotted line below each one, write why you rated yourself that way. BE HONEST!

I hide my risk-taking behaviors from others.

_____
0 (Not Much)   5 (A Little)   10 (A Great Deal)

I avoid friends and family in favor of risk-taking events.

_____
0 (Not Much)   5 (A Little)   10 (A Great Deal)

I always have my next adrenaline rush on my mind.

_____
0 (Not Much)   5 (A Little)   10 (A Great Deal)

If I don't experience an adrenaline rush, I feel physically ill.

_____
0 (Not Much)   5 (A Little)   10 (A Great Deal)

I have financial and occupational troubles due to my risk-taking behavior.

_____
0 (Not Much)   5 (A Little)   10 (A Great Deal)

The HIGHER your score on each of the options above, the more of a problem you have in the specific aspect measured by the assessment. Areas where you scored low suggest that you are not experiencing many signs of a risky behavior addiction in those areas.

Will life change if you overcome your addiction to risky behavior?

_____
0 (Not Much)   5 (A Little)   10 (A Great Deal)

Do you want to change your current risk-taking habits?

_____
0 (Not Much)   5 (A Little)   10 (A Great Deal)

Quotes about Addiction to Risky Behavior

Read all three of the quotations below.

#1

Peer pressure is just that: pressure.
~ Jerry Spinelli

#2

The busyness of life can keep you running from one activity to the next.
If you never step back to consider whether all those activities are really how you
want to spend your time, you could miss out on building the kind of life you want.
Devote at least 10 minutes each day to examining the bigger picture in your life.
~ Amy Morin

#3

Fitness is really important for my mental and emotional
equilibrium as well as my physical wellbeing.
~ Robert Rinder

Pick a quote that sounds like you and explain why. #_____

_____

_____

Pick one that inspires you to do better and explain how you will do that. #_____

_____

_____

Pick a quote that taught you something and explain what it taught you. #_____

_____

_____

Write your very own quote regarding risk-prevention behaviors.

_____

_____

_____

_____

_____

_____

_____

WholePerson

Whole Person Associates is the leading publisher of training
resources for professionals who empower people to create and
maintain healthy lifestyles. Our creative resources will help
you work effectively with your clients in the areas
of stress management, wellness promotion,
mental health, and life skills.

Please visit us at our website: **WholePerson.com**.
You can check out our entire line of products, place an order,
request our print catalog, and sign up for our monthly
special notifications.

Whole Person Associates
800-247-6789
Books@WholePerson.com

CPSIA information can be obtained
at www.ICGtesting.com
Printed in the USA
BVHW020301240223
659120BV00005B/15